THE DUALITY OF THE

Modern Woman

THE DUALITY OF THE
Modern Woman

Free Yourself from the Restraints of Culture, Shame, and
Judgement to Embrace Your Femininity and Wild Side

BY JENNIFER LUDINGTON

gatekeeper press™

Columbus, Ohio

The Duality of the Modern Woman: Free Yourself from the Restraints of Culture, Shame, and Judgement to *Embrace Your Femininity and Wild Side*

Published by Gatekeeper Press

2167 Stringtown Rd, Suite 109

Columbus, OH 43123-2989

www.GatekeeperPress.com

The editorial work for this book is entirely the product of the author. Gatekeeper Press did not participate in and is not responsible for any aspect of this element.

Library of Congress Control Number: 2021939132

ISBN (paperback): 9781662913761

eISBN: 9781662913778

I am an "old school" feminist, born out of the consciousness-raising circles of the early 1970's and shaped by the influence of Betty Friedan, Bella Abzug, and Gloria Steinem. My doctoral dissertation, written in 1995, was "The Future of Feminism: Where Do We Go From Here"?

This book is a collaboration of over 30 women's stories and points of view that seeks to answer and expand upon that question. What does it mean to be a modern woman and how does one express her "outside the box" needs for expression? Jennifer Ludington has lovingly curated these stories and added her own "Duality Dare" section at the end of each chapter to encourage the reader to dig deep into her own experience and discover herself anew. Roll up your sleeves, reader. You've got work to do!

- Dr. Judith Rich, Speaker, Trainer, Coach, and
Bestselling Author of *Beyond The Box*

CONTENTS

WHO IS THE MODERN WOMAN?

As modern women, we've lost ourselves, and it's time to get us back.

It's time to rediscover what we as modern women bring to the table...not as women trying to be men in a patriarchal culture, but as women who embrace our feminine qualities and use them to create the lives we love. Lives that feel authentic to us instead of lives modeled around external expectations and cultural norms that society decided are right for us.

Our values and our gifts have been lost in a patriarchal culture that emphasizes the masculine energy, and have taught us to label our natrual feminine ways of being and doing as wrong.

From our inception, we're faced with adversity. There are systemic ways we've been denied the same rights as men, from our ancestral lineage and even beyond. I believe when women are fully in their divine feminine, only then can we alchemize adversity into empathy.

We endure things men have no idea how to (naturally) endure, but that's not to say we should judge or lump men into one negative category. That's not what this book is about. I love men. The vast majority of men are beautiful, soulful beings who care about equality and shifting the antiquated paradigm that does not do women justice. For these narratives to shift, it requires us all, as humans, to be purposeful and unified in our pursuit of an upgraded outlook on how the modern woman is accepted and integrated into new social norms.

Part of my mission is to encourage more of us women to step up, stand up, and speak up, so we can lead with powerful voices and create the change we want to see in the world. As a collective, I would love to see us support each other so we can embrace all sides of us, instead of being confined to the stereotypes of being just one thing. No one is just one thing. When we allow ourselves the freedom to shift, and recreate our identity as we see fit, however often we see fit, that's when we pave the way for our sisters to do the same.

Our culture has created boxes we feel we have to live in--who we should be and how we should show up. If we don't be or show up in those "culturally" acceptable ways, we're stereotyped as bitches, or as over-emotional, or as ballbusters, or any other number of labels meant to pigeon-hole us into just one thing.

So how do we shift that? How do we live into and celebrate all sides of ourselves, instead of making who we authentically are wrong because it's not a cultural norm, or "acceptable," or "virtuous?"

Can we tap into the connection with ourselves and with other women? Can we tap into the empathy we intrinsically embody because of the adversity we face? Can we run companies, crush goals, break glass ceilings, and still be accepted, loved, and approved of?

Can we do all that and still run our household, love our children, nurture our husbands, and allow men to open doors for us? Can we feel okay with ourselves being in all those roles?

I believe we get to.

I believe we get to accept that not everything we do has to be perfect. Perfection is a paradigm I believe we get to permanently delete from our language.

Our journey doesn't have to end up exactly where we thought it "should," or the way past generations have done it.

I believe we get to tap into our sexuality without being labeled as "bad girls." I believe we can expose our sensuality and femininity without being shamed or labeled a slut.

I believe we get to tap into our true, natural intuition without being labeled a "witch." (Although, a good witch is something I can 100% get behind!)

We get to hold our shield and be the heroes of our own lives. We get to find and embrace our duality in all its forms.

That, to me, is what it means to be a modern, in demand woman.

WHAT IS DUALITY?

This book is about the duality that exists inside the modern woman, and it's about the contrast that exists within all of us.

We have the contrast--the polarity--of the feminine and the masculine. We have dark and light both, because, without the dark, there is no light.

Our ascension happens when we stop resisting all sides of ourselves and instead accept all sides of ourselves.

Personally, these different sides of me always felt like they conflicted with one another. I felt connected to the light-hearted, carefree hippie side of me who loves crystals, oracle cards, meditation, and yoga.

Then I had this strict military side that was driven, masculine, forceful, goal-oriented, and competitive.

Some days I wanted to generate, perform, run up mountains and crush goals. Other days I wanted to read, meditate, snuggle with my kids and dogs, and do yoga.

There were days I showed up in all my feminine sensuality and sexuality. There were also days where I showed up as a nurturing, loving, tender mom. There were days I wanted to wear high heels, red lipstick, and a sexy outfit, and also days where I wanted to lounge in sweats, with my hair wrapped up in a messy bun.

I couldn't quite figure out where the middle was, and anything I thought might be the middle felt messy, and someplace I didn't belong. I felt like I was always showing up inauthentically.

That changed as I learned to accept all sides of myself. I allowed myself to shift and mold day to day, minute to minute, even moment to moment, and when I did that, that's when I truly found freedom.

I stopped shrinking myself, hiding, and quieting my voice. I let go of cultural expectations around who and what I should be. I let go of the shame I had around that sexual energy I embodied so easily. I let go of the "good girl" image we're supposed to live into, and instead lived into what was true for me. I aligned in my feminine and my masculine. I aligned in my light and my dark. I had so much duality. There was shame and pride, humility and ego. There was a mom/wife and entrepreneur.

Modern women are transformers. We flow, shift, and change. We mold and adapt and are brave and scared, all simultaneously.

MY DUALITY

Before going further, let me tell you a little about who I am and what I'm about.

My name's Jennifer Ludington, but I'm known as Jen the JENerator. I'm a Mind Ascension coach, best-selling author, keynote speaker, accomplished athlete, and most recently, co-host of the Soul Ascends podcast.

I've spent over fifteen years coaching over one thousand clients into their own authentic, value-centered lives, and I now know that the power of authentic connection to your truth is the only way to set yourself free.

I'm also the daughter of a thirty-year, special ops, Sergeants Major Marine Corps father and a happy-to-be-free, loving, artist, free-spirited hippie mom. The polarity of my parents makes me laugh! Could they be any more different?

The duality I faced growing up with the grit, resilience, hard work, and structure of my father was the polar opposite of my mother's fun-loving free spirit, and lack of responsibility. Honestly, she was a "head in the clouds" mom who modeled sexuality based on being one of the most beautiful women I've ever seen.

Coming from that, I always felt pulled and stuck in the confusing middle of my duality. I belonged nowhere. I was sometimes called inauthentic because I could easily shift from one side of my duality to the other.

I could run grueling races and do other gritty, physical things with my body (that really were just a mental game). I was tough as nails in some areas.

In other areas, I'm super sexual, sensual, nurturing, and even jovial, and all at the same time.

Having a decorated Marine for a father, I was taught the importance of grit and resolve from an early age. At one point, it took me in a direction I didn't expect.

I became an exercise addict, and eventually developed several eating disorders, including anorexia and bulimia. I was obsessed with being "fitness perfect." It was one of many masks I hid behind.

From the outside, I was an extremely successful elite fitness studio owner. I appeared to be a sleek, sexy and strong bikini competitor. I had the body our society and culture tell us reflects health and success.

5

But in reality, I wasn't all that healthy, physically or emotionally. I was drowning in a river of shame and deceit. I was disconnected from my truth, afraid and unable to use my voice.

A big part of that was because I didn't understand how to embrace my duality, though the duality in myself always intrigued me.

Once I embraced all that I am, and grew into the modern day woman, I returned to whom I forgot to be...to the me I was before outside expectations and who I thought I "should" be eclipsed me.

My breakthrough didn't come because my health was on the brink, with my thyroid at an all-time low, my hair falling out in clumps, and not having a period for years. Nor were autoimmune disease and chronic insomnia enough to make me change course.

My breakthrough came via my daughter. It's often said that our children teach us our greatest lessons, and that couldn't be truer for me.

As a single mom, my daughter and I were closer than the average duo. One night at the dinner table, when she was about seven years old, Lainee asked, "Mommy, have you ever eaten anything other than lettuce?"

I broke down. I realized I'd been modeling this dangerous striving, hustle hard, perfectionist behavior to my young daughter. I had to shift—if not for me, for her. For some of us, we can literally self-destruct without the slightest nudge to change before we do serious damage. Others (me included) need an outside force strong enough to stop them from hitting rock bottom.

For me, and so many others, there was and never could be a more powerful why than our children. After Lainee asked me whether I'd ever eaten anything other than lettuce, my action led me to break through. I decided to sharpen my sword and slay those damn dragons once and for all, and that's what I did.

Part of that journey was stepping more and more into my duality. As I did, I realized that the duality never ends. Meaning, I'm a shapeshifter, and so are the modern women I see around me. We shape and shift and become what we need to become in the moment.

One moment we are nurturing and compassionate and loving and giving with our kids. The next moment we're expected to show up as sexpots in our high heels and lingerie for our intimate partners. We're expected to keep a Pilates-looking body while running multi-million dollar businesses. We're CEOs of companies running the PTA and being chauffeurs to our kids, volunteering for our daughter's volleyball teams, and all the other hats we get to wear.

We get to be whomever we want to be. It's our gift but also our challenge. How do we find what's right for us when we're expected to be all the things all the time? Yes, we can have it all, but does that mean we should? Especially when it may not even be our version of "all?"

We're flooded with phony body images Photoshopped to make us believe that's what we're supposed to look like. We're shown images of perfect families where the kids go to Ivy League schools, framed by white picket fences glistening against a well-manicured lawn, with homes decorated like something out of a Martha Stewart magazine. We are force-fed this lifestyle porn, and anything else is less-than.

How do we find our own authenticity when we're bombarded with unattainable standards and made to feel less-than every day we haven't achieved them?

How do we find our real truth? Our own alignment? How do we know what it means to be a modern woman?

Did you know that women are wired for pleasure? It's not just a "nice to have" bonus after serving, giving, and nurturing our loved ones. It's our strength. It's our secret superpower, and when we dive into it unapologetically, we can harness our shield and our sword.

We are meant to receive all the pleasure, desire, joy, and fun available for us. But do we even really know what pleasure means anymore? Do we know what brings us joy? Hope? Fulfillment? Do we really know what will set our soul on fire?

Or are you, like so many women in today's world, getting lost in the middle because you think you can't be all sides of yourself?

In this book, I challenge you to rediscover how you're performing. Are you performing for culture and expectations, or are you performing for your own pleasure, desires, and intrinsic values?

We lost our pleasure somewhere along the way, and I want to help you rediscover it. I want to help you remember who you really are.

HOW TO PUT THIS BOOK INTO ACTION

In the stories you will read in this book, you'll see many ways to tap into our inner knowing--into that ancestral wisdom we, as women, hold in our bones.

In these stories, you'll meet shield maidens, goddesses, and givers of life. These women inspire me, and I hope they will inspire you.

As you read their stories, look for the contrast. You'll see their fear and their bravery, their feminine and their masculine, and their shame and their pride. You'll see their ego and their humility, their light and their dark. There's contrast in everything.

The best way to use this book is to dive in and allow yourself to be absorbed by these women's stories. See where you can pull out your own duality. See where you can remember your wild and return to the ancestral knowing of who you really BE...the person you may forget to remember that you are.

I want this book to be interactive for you and support you by giving you stories of incredible women who have forged their own path...women who've created lives of pleasure and joy, fulfillment and

8

ease. Let their stories be guides to find your own way. Get curious about what matters to you, and what sets your soul on fire.

I've placed Duality Dares after each chapter, complete with journal pages at the back of this book, to help you dive deeper at your own pace. They're designed to help you find the joy, the fulfillment, and the spark you had before the world told you who to be...back when you didn't shrink yourself, and you allowed yourself to fully show up for who you are.

Dare yourself to desire again. Dare yourself to perform for your own pleasure versus the expectations of the external world. Dare yourself to dive into your values, your truth, and your inner knowing.

Allow the contrast to guide you to accept it. Whichever side you land on, fully show up for it. Whatever that duality is, live into it, fight for it, honor it, respect it, nurture it, and give it pleasure. Let yourself receive all the desires you truly want.

Bring these into your intimate settings into your home, your car, on your hikes, maybe at the gym, when you can be with your thoughts.

I hope this book opens something for you...a way for you to dive deeper into what is authentic for you. I hope it helps you become curious about who you are as a modern woman--how you want to show up, what brings you joy and pleasure, and how to find ease and flow in your day to day--not in all the doing, but in whom you get to BE.

I've added a journal to the back of this book, so you can keep your journey all in one place. Have a pen handy when you read this book, so you can implement your Duality Dares as you go.

HOW TO GET YOUR FREE GIFT

As a thank you for investing in this book, I want to give you a special gift: Full, unedited video interviews featuring the ladies whose stories you're about to read. Hearing these interviews in their entirety will give you even more insight in your own duality. See these women, listen to their stories, and use the gift in each story to dive even deeper and rediscover who you were always meant to be.

To claim your free gift, head to www.thedualityofthemodern woman.com/gift. Enter your email address when prompted, and I'll give you free access to these goodies:

- Full, uncut video interviews with every person featured in this book

- Videos for every Duality Dare, where I expand on every Dare and share tips to getting the absolute most out of it

- A special invitation to join my private community

I hope the full versions of these stories inspire you the way they've inspired me. I hope they shed light into the dark corners, bring about awareness, and serve as rocket fuel for your ascension.

Use this book, and these interviews, to create awareness around who you are outside the box you've been stuffed into.

Join me at www.thedualityofthemodernwoman.com/gift so I can support you on this journey.

CHAPTER 1

INTUITION
MEGAN MCCANN

Megan McCann is a bestselling author, speaker coach, podcast co-host of the Soul Ascend Podcast, and founder of Soul Success. This global personal development brand brings female leaders together to align in business and spirituality.

I came into this world feeling like I was different from a lot of other kids. I had this burning desire to do things that seemed outside of the box. I always loved entrepreneurship--making something out of nothing.

I also loved the idea of full freedom to do whatever I wanted, instead of somebody else telling me what I had to do as a career. I even thought about that as a young girl--how I would be my own boss.

But as I got older, I fell into comparison and self-sabotage. I started down a path so out of alignment with who I really am.

I got a master's degree. I worked corporate. Then I became a teacher, then a counselor. I always went back to what cultural expectations said I should do, including once I became a mom. I felt like I had to fit within this box, because there's so much pressure now to do it right.

All these different things I've tried brought me back to who I've always been--somebody who's of service, somebody who loves communities, somebody who loves networking. That's my zone of genius, and that's where Soul Success was born.

The future is female, and the power is in women locking arms and owning our divine feminine.

HOW DO YOU DEFINE A MODERN WOMAN?

The modern day woman taps into her intuition and divine feminine. We have thousands of years of women silencing their voices and doing what they should be doing to fit inside the box of what's expected of us.

Listening to our intuition is one of the greatest powers women have. When we have a mission or a purpose, or something that's driving us, we're listening to that instead of to all the voices outside of us or the conversations in our head telling us what we should and should not do.

"Go to work. Don't go to work. Stay home. Raise the kids. No, you should have a career."

If staying at home and raising the kids is you listening to your intuition, and doing those things lights you up, beautiful.

But if you're a woman who wants something else--like a career or a business--that's beautiful, too.

I've met a lot of women who know that in pursuing their passion, their Dharma, their dreams, they're contributing not just to themselves but to everyone else around them, including their children.

The modern day woman doesn't fit inside one box. She's not just the career driven woman, she's not just the stay-at-home mom. She's whatever she wants to be. She figures it out, imperfectly, and she's okay with that.

IN WHAT AREAS OF YOUR LIFE HAVE YOU STEPPED OUT OF CULTURAL NORMS, DEFIED THEM, OR GONE AGAINST THEM? AND IN THOSE AREAS OF YOUR LIFE WHERE YOU'VE DONE THAT, HAVE YOU EXPERIENCED ANY SHAME OR GUILT, EITHER EXTERNAL OR INTERNAL? IF SO, HOW DID YOU MANAGE THAT?

When I had my first daughter, my business was built, and it was doing well, but all I wanted was to be a present parent, so my husband and I took time off for two years to do that.

With our second child, it was a different experience. I still wanted to have those first days with her, yet I was excited to work because I had a big mission.

Another way: I listen to my intuition instead of doing what others expect or what my logical mind says.

There's a distinction between intuition and the logical mind. Your intuition says, "This thought keeps coming up, and it feels terrific. And I don't know how it's going to work yet, but it feels good."

The logical mind is the part that comes in with a million reasons it's impossible for you.

When there's something inside you with a burning desire to make an impact, and that's your contribution to other people, your logical mind says, "Well, there's no way you can monetize that. There's no way it's going to work."

What I recommend is having a conversation with the self-sabotage. Write down every single limiting belief your logical mind has around your desire. Then ask, "How does that feel?"

The more you do this, the more you'll notice how often you endure those limiting thoughts every single day.

Your thoughts create momentum. They either pull you towards your desires or push you away from your desires.

HOW DO YOU TAP INTO YOUR DIVINE FEMININE AND WILD SIDE EACH DAY?

When I built my first business, I had to outperform my own self-limiting beliefs and prove I was not a nobody. That came with hustling, that came with masculine energy, that came with more numbers, more people. I was doing all the things other people were doing to be successful.

I did this for two and a half years. In year three, I burnt the fuck out, and I stopped working. That was me and my masculine, and it was not sustainable.

As women, we are not designed to be masculine for long periods. It serves its purpose for short periods of time, but eventually, you burn out.

That's why it's critical to slow down, go outside, connect to nature, use crystals, meditate--whatever you need to do to slow down and listen to what's going on inside.

Pay attention to your thoughts, your feelings, your emotions. That, to me, is tapping into the feminine. That's where the portals open to receive the downloads that are part of why we're here.

Quantum leaps cannot happen with hustle. If you want to multiply your income, if you want to manifest love, if you want something you've never created before, that doesn't come with the masculine. That comes by slowing down and listening to what your intuition is saying.

How do I really feel at this moment? Where do I feel inspired? It doesn't feel forced anymore when you do that. It just flows right through you.

Yes, we do need the masculine because we do need to get into action. We do need a strategy. We do need to implement tools. But if we're always running, running, running, eventually, we'll exhaust ourselves.

DUALITY DARE

Intuition

The logical mind is the masculine side of our polarity. Our intuition and inner knowing are the creative divine feminine side of our polarity. We use both sides daily to make decisions, and our decisions add up quickly. They can create alignment, or they can create disharmony.

In our current "hustle hard," "Boss babe" culture society, we're programmed to rely on our masculine. We also get more acknowledgement when we operate from our masculine go-go-go energy. But constantly operating in masculine energy leads to burnout, and fast.

In this Duality Dare, I want you to experiment. Identify a small daily decision. (Start small!) Then allow yourself to ease into deciphering between logical masculine and intuitive feminine. This will help you relearn to trust your inner knowing (aka intuition).

What's one choice you can make today from your intuition? Maybe it's as simple as how you drive to work, what you wear, or which workout class you choose.

The point is to practice with these small decisions to learn to trust your intuition for the bigger decisions in your life, versus only relying on your masculine logical side.

For your Duality Dare, do this by asking yourself, "How does this decision make me feel? Does it feel like force or flow?

If the decision gives you a nudge of ease in your gut (solar plexus), or if you just have a "feeling," then follow it before your logical mind (masculine) can talk you out of it.

Now evaluate. Was your intuition accurate? How do you know? Did you hit all the green lights on your way to work? Did you get tons of compliments on your new dress? Did you rock it out in dance class or feel like a goddess during yoga?

This is all evidence for your self-trust. Your divine feminine is worthy of acknowledgement, and she deserves a seat at the decision-making table. Give her a chance, and I think you'll be pleasantly surprised by how much deep wisdom she holds, and the undeniable joy she can bring to your life.

CHAPTER 2

DOORS
MONICK HALM

Monick Halm is a best-selling author, educator, and the founder of Real Estate Investor Goddesses. Monick's mission is to help one million women create financial freedom through real estate investing, and do so in a feminine way.

Real Estate Investor Goddesses came to me as a divine download, during an amazing conference about how you build wealth. Looking around the room, there were one-hundred-twenty people, and only eight were women. Two of those women weren't even attendees. They were in the back working.

And it just came to me: Bring women into this room and build wealth in a feminine way.

I started out as an attorney. I was miserable, but I ignored it, and kept trying to work harder. That's when I had the most terrible repercussions (like ending up in the hospital with shingles and a ruptured appendix).

When I listened to my intuition--that divine guidance--and surrendered to it, everything changed. I learned to pleasure through and create sisterhood instead of hustle and grind and co-create with the men around me.

I've studied the divine feminine since 2004, and I want to work with women who resonate with a goddess, though I think we're all goddesses. We all have at least a drop of the Divine within us.

Some women resonate with a goddess, and other women think, "I don't know about goddesses." That's fine if it doesn't resonate with someone, but if it doesn't, she's not my person. And that's okay.

HOW DO YOU DEFINE A MODERN WOMAN?

Being a modern woman is getting to define a modern woman however you want to. For so long, we as women had these prescribed roles. There were a lot of things we couldn't be or do.

For example, until 1974, many women couldn't have their own bank account. Women couldn't get their own credit by themselves without a male cosigner until 1988. In certain states, a woman could not get a business loan without a male relative cosigner.

As modern women, we have this freedom, and the challenge with that is, sometimes we feel that because we can have it all, we have to try for it all, which creates a lot of burnout, depression, rage, and eating disorders.

We've also been taught to show up in the masculine, which is often about winning and competition, and no pain, no gain. But we have a lot of opportunities when we approach life through the feminine.

My mission is to help one million women create financial freedom through real estate. But I want to teach them how to do it through the divine feminine. When you're showing up from the true mature feminine, it's so powerful. It's not about the hustle and grind; it's about the pleasure and flow.

Discover what brings you pleasure because the feminine is wired for pleasure. List at least thirty things that are pleasurable for you. Include at least one of them in your day, every day.

IN WHAT AREAS OF YOUR LIFE HAVE YOU STEPPED OUT OF CULTURAL NORMS, DEFIED THEM, OR GONE AGAINST THEM? AND IN THOSE AREAS OF YOUR LIFE WHERE YOU'VE DONE THAT, HAVE YOU EXPERIENCED ANY SHAME OR GUILT, EITHER EXTERNAL OR INTERNAL? IF SO, HOW DID YOU MANAGE THAT?

Definitely approaching real estate investing in a feminine way. I also approach my work in a feminine way.

For example, when you find yourself blocked in your work, the masculine way is to man up and muscle through. The feminine way is to pleasure through, or take a pleasure break and come back feeling pleasured. Then things seem to open up.

If you really can't take a pleasure break, figure out how to add pleasure to what you're doing. If you have to commute and don't like the long drive, turn on your favorite music, audiobook, or podcast. Bring a friend with you. If you have to wash dishes, put on a tiara, your favorite music, and a belly dancing skirt.

If you're doing something that isn't pleasurable, only do it if it's leading to a pleasurable result. If it's not, stop. There's no point.

Money is another area where I've stepped outside cultural norms. Money will come in, or not come in, in exact proportion to the energy we feel around it. As women, when we are creating and showing up in pleasure, that's when we can create the most money.

For a long time, I had this avoidant relationship with money. I had tons of money issues.

19

When I started showing up in gratitude for money, and toward creditors, and even bills, my husband and I went from $60,000 in credit card debt to $600,000 in the bank in sixty-six weeks.

Everything that went out was a symbol of the inexhaustible supply of the universe, and ten times as much as goes out is on its way to me.

HOW DO YOU TAP INTO YOUR DIVINE FEMININE AND WILD SIDE EACH DAY?

We embody both the masculine and the feminine, and it's important to honor both. Otherwise, we're all yin and no yang.

A few years ago, I decided I wasn't going to take any action at all for a full year. I'd been grinding, and I decided to be in flow the whole year. It felt really good, and the most incredible things showed up. I'd really want to work with a certain person, and that person would call me and hire me. It was a wild year.

After that year, I realized I needed to take more action, but I approached it completely differently. My mantra became "inspired action, orgasmic results."

As in, I don't have to take action unless I'm inspired to take action, but when I am inspired to take action, I do have to take action. And then, wow!

When I approached it that way, I created an energetic space of pleasure, which feels good.

I wanted and asked for what I desired, and it manifested, instead of me having to grind and force it.

A part of me takes action, and I've embraced that masculine part of me. But it's not what I lead with anymore.

DUALITY DARE

Doors

In my programs and coaching, I speak into what I call Value Endurance. My definition of Value Endurance is enduring only that which aligns with your intrinsic core values and brings you closer to your desired result.

What are you enduring? Are you enduring just for the simple fact of going through the motions, day in and day out? Are you enduring for a big purpose, vision and passion? Is your vision in alignment with your core values; and are you performing your tasks for your own pleasure and purpose?

Monick speaks to creating pleasure in the unpleasurable. This vision is your north star, so how can you realign all of your behaviors and "actions" to reach your desired result in pleasure?

For example, to create a real estate portfolio but don't love crunching numbers and creating spreadsheets, how can you be creative in this step? Can you buy yourself a fancy new executive portfolio and bedazzle it? Can you surround yourself with candles that smell delicious? Can you play your favorite music? Can you create a specialty coffee drink you only get to drink when you are deep in detailed work?

In this Duality Dare, I would like you to identify the big vision and what you're creating.

Identify the steps that are necessary but don't necessarily bring you pleasure. In the journal portion, write down five ways you can bring pleasure to the unpleasurable, so you can cultivate Value Endurance in your daily life, and ultimately reach your desired result with joy, fulfillment and ease. Adding pleasure is key to tapping into your divine feminine.

CHAPTER 3

JEALOUSY
SARA CONNELL

Sara Connell is an author and writing coach. She's been featured on Oprah, Good Morning America, The View, and in Forbes magazine.

I started in a job where I was sexually abused every day. I was numbing that pain with eating disorder behavior. There were all kinds of really traumatic, challenging things with which I wasn't dealing.

Then I read a book I found randomly in an airport, and everything in my life changed. I didn't just read the book and put it back.

That book was the catalyst for me to leave the job, get help with my health, and start leaving abusive relationships in general in my life, which was a pattern from childhood. It also inspired me to pursue my dream of being a writer.

I discovered I have the incredible gift of helping other women who have a mission, or a story they know they need to share, bring it to the world, whether it's through a book, the stage, or however they're sharing it.

I do it because I was that person who was dying, but because one woman courageously, unflinchingly, shared her story, I am here today.

It's such a big deal to discuss women and how we are showing up in the world. The models that a lot of us were taught growing up don't work, and they bring us to break down in every way: Mentally, spiritually, emotionally, and physically.

HOW DO YOU DEFINE A MODERN WOMAN?

For a long time, it meant hustle or working hard. I am really into breaking down the patriarchy model. Not men, not women, just a masculine leadership model not in alignment with me as a modern woman.

Being a modern woman, to me, means being a ten out of ten in my relationship with my son, my husband, my friends, my clients, and myself.

I love abundance. I love making money. I love helping other people make money. It's fabulous because of the freedom and joy that it can bring us.

But part of being a modern woman today is that I am driven by my authenticity and my soul versus my head, which might get into many more sort of ego types of motivations. It's important to find what's authentic to you.

My favorite way to tell when someone is in their heart versus their head is to ask, "what lights you up?"

Our being will have what you could call resonance. When you see someone doing something, or saying something like, "Oh, that's how I knew I had to write a book. I had to be an author." I look for what buzzes.

That buzzing shows up in surprising ways. I'd see certain people, and I would almost be vibrating, including if the emotion was jealousy. I see jealousy as an indicator--as a preview of what we're meant to be.

It's a coming attraction of something we haven't yet allowed ourselves to be. We locate our own greatness in other people.

If you see something in someone, it means you have the potential. That's your coming attraction. That's your next step.

I get to lock arms with this person I'm jealous of and say," Thank you for being a guide, to show me what I'm here to do next."

We need not be in the "compare and despair" competition trap. If I compete, I feel less than. I feel like, "What's the point?" Versus, "Oh, this is leading me."

IN WHAT AREAS OF YOUR LIFE HAVE YOU STEPPED OUT OF CULTURAL NORMS, DEFIED THEM, OR GONE AGAINST THEM? AND IN THOSE AREAS OF YOUR LIFE WHERE YOU'VE DONE THAT, HAVE YOU EXPERIENCED ANY SHAME OR GUILT, EITHER EXTERNAL OR INTERNAL? IF SO, HOW DID YOU MANAGE THAT?

I run my entire business through my intuition. That does not mean I don't listen and learn strategy, or study great teachers, but I do not make a choice unless it passes the intuition test.

I had someone recently present me with a really exciting opportunity. I got very excited, but my whole body and my gut were saying, not right now.

It was nothing about her or the opportunity. It just wasn't for right now.

In logical business, the norm would be, if someone creates a great business idea and it's aligned and reputable, take it. But every time I've ignored those signals and signs in myself, it hasn't worked out well. That's a very feminine leadership kind of thing versus a masculine model. Since I've started running my business through my intuition, my business has doubled or tripled every year.

For me, I play the game of, "what lets me know this is aligned with my intuition?" I would start paying attention to physical sensations. I would get a low, dull feeling, an anxious feeling low in my belly. I realized that was my body and my intuition saying this is not a green light.

I also paid attention to my heart. Does this light me up, or is it just something I think I should do or think is a good idea?

HOW DO YOU TAP INTO YOUR DIVINE FEMININE AND WILD SIDE EACH DAY?

I didn't connect to that part of me for my whole upbringing. I had this moment in my late 20s where I said, "Oh, my God, I'm just behaving like a man. I have no connection to the feminine," and it was a startling and upsetting wake up call.

That connection is something important and precious. I'm a big meditator because I am very high octane and have intensity, which I love. I love that I'm passionate. The meditation calms me down in that sort of softer place. I can access a more relaxed sort of goddess energy.

I'm also big into yoga. Something about the flow and the pool, it's powerful and really precious to me. I make time for it no matter what. If I have to get up super early, that's happening at least once a week.

I've done all kinds of things to explore over the years with friends who are brilliant at things like chanting and belly dancing. If a friend is putting on a workshop for somebody, I'm going. I remember taking a painting class once where we got to roll in the paint and get the paint all over.

I identify with wolf energy. If you've read Clarissa Pinkola Estés, she writes a lot about these Tales of the Wild Woman Within, and I love her work. I love that whole idea. There's a lightness to it. It's a gift to everyone because it forms our creativity and our business genius.

DUALITY DARE
Jealousy

Jealousy--the coming attraction reel for the next level of your life. After extracting this nugget from Sara's interview, my brain went down a rabbit hole. This concept is really, truly radical if applied. Could those twinges of jealousy and resonance be the universe preparing me for my next step?

What if you allowed yourself to fully believe this concept was irrevocably true for every single tiny itty bitty twinge of jealousy you have ever felt or will ever feel? Wow!

Can you be open enough to believe this is equally just as possible as it is impossible? What if, you manifested through your jealousy a highlight reel of everything and anything you have ever wanted?

For your Duality Dare, I want you to be honest and write down three things in the journal section you're feeling at least a little twinge of jealousy about.

Now write down three things you have manifested (created) in your life right now. Then go back through your history and see if you can find a moment when you were jealous of other people who had or were doing what you have or are doing.

This exercise anchored me to the proof that jealousy is the highlight reel for what's to come. I was jealous of one of my mentors' beach houses about four years ago. I would see her abundance and get that little nudge of wanting what she had. Every time she went live on social media on top of her beach house rooftop overlooking the ocean, I felt that jealousy kick in.

I wanted to hear ocean waves at night. I wanted to create memories on the beach with my kids and grandchildren, just like my mom and grandmother did with me. I wanted to feel the sand in my toes every day, and wake up to the smell of salt in the air.

This year I bought a beach house. Literally a beach house. The girl that was flat broke, a single mom, unable to buy milk for her daughter, living in her friend's basement, unable to afford gas, without a college degree. That girl now owns a beach house.

My feelings of jealousy were my highlight reel. The jealousy supported me in manifesting my wildest dreams.

When you open yourself up to possibility, and you allow yourself to believe that the impossible is possible, your breakthrough is on the other side of your jealousy.

CHAPTER 4

RESPONSIBILITY
JESSICA PEREZ-BEEBE

Jessica Perez-Beebe is a pro athlete and performance coach for entrepreneurs who want to hit their next level of performance. Her Proven Pro Mindset system helps entrepreneurs adopt the habits and visualizations used by professional athletes. She's been an entrepreneur for 16 years and founded four companies from the ground up.

I had this huge wake-up call when my mother was suddenly killed in a car accident at age 45. When you're in your 20s, that seems kind of far away. I felt like I was just getting started.

I knew I wanted to work for myself. I knew I wanted to create something, and have the freedom and not feel constrained.

I was in a job I didn't like, but I stayed because it was paying good money. Every time I went to leave, I got a raise, and that sucked me back in. Everyone told me, you're just so lucky to have this great job.

On the inside, I wasn't happy. I wasn't doing something I was great at. When my mother died and I got my wake-up call, that was my leg into entrepreneurship. I took that big leap and never looked back.

I was in the health and fitness industry for a long time. In 2015 I sold my gym, and I'm proud that the business is still growing and flourishing.

About a year after selling it, I was hired as a consultant and success coach for a Fortune 500 company that coaches fitness entrepreneurs.

You can only consult for so long before your entrepreneur's brain wants to create, so that's when I got into the online space. I took a year and trained with Tony Robbins, got certified, and started my online coaching company about three and a half years ago.

HOW DO YOU DEFINE A MODERN WOMAN?

Modern means to show up, be visible, contribute, and take yourself on. Get the education, training, and mentorship required to show up and be a leader who can be authentic, pass on wisdom and be an inspiration.

Women have been expected to handle so much, even when not working. Work adds a whole other dimension. It changes the dynamic in your family.

My clients need help with overwhelm and expectations because they want the opposite. Just because you're a high performer and successful does not mean you're not having challenges in your personal life.

What spins most entrepreneurs out of control is focusing on what they do and how they do it. When you get caught up in the mechanics, you're disconnected from why you were doing this.

When you're connected and grounded in your purpose, and you've got that clear vision, you're not bound by time. It's not a two or three-year thing.

Overwhelm is a symptom of not having simple productivity tools set up, so you manage your day and have boundaries. You're not operating off a long to do list, trying to accomplish everything in one day or even a year.

Realize at the end of the day, or even the end of your life, you're not going to lie there saying, I'm so glad I worked sixteen hours every day.

IN WHAT AREAS OF YOUR LIFE HAVE YOU STEPPED OUT OF CULTURAL NORMS, DEFIED THEM, OR GONE AGAINST THEM? AND IN THOSE AREAS OF YOUR LIFE WHERE YOU'VE DONE THAT, HAVE YOU EXPERIENCED ANY SHAME OR GUILT, EITHER EXTERNAL OR INTERNAL? IF SO, HOW DID YOU MANAGE THAT?

I'm sick of hearing you need to be more in your feminine. People have a duality. Sometimes, you will be operating more in your masculine. Other times, you will be operating more in your feminine. You can learn when to turn it on and off on any given day. It's a pendulum. It's not going to be static.

However, for a woman, it's draining to spend all your time in your masculine. I do think if a woman is feeling burned out, if you're feeling overwhelmed, if you have those moments, then ask yourself, "When's the last time I really let myself receive?" Because you probably need to go a little heavy on that for the next couple days, maybe the next week.

For me, I get this stuff on my schedule. I love my work, and I could literally just keep going, so time to receive has to get on my schedule.

My assistant knows, block this, block that. If someone wants to get on my calendar, the answer is no, and I don't care who it is. They can say they're my friend--it doesn't matter. Do not book anything. I even put my dates and my family time on the calendar. It's all about setting those boundaries.

HOW DO YOU TAP INTO YOUR DIVINE FEMININE AND WILD SIDE EACH DAY?

I put on heels and the tiny bikini, get on stage in front of hundreds of thousands of people, strut my stuff. Most of the time, I win medals.

You can say it's a little combination of masculine and feminine, but it's a little wild, right? I'm putting myself out there.

So many people are worried about what other people think. It's one thing that holds women back. "What are people gonna think of me?"

What I've figured out is that people will judge you and make assumptions about you no matter what.

They'll judge you because you're a physique athlete. People made assumptions about me when I was a competitive CrossFit athlete and when I was overweight and smoking cigarettes in my twenties. Either way, people will make assumptions and judgments.

I know what I want, I know who I am, and I know why I compete. I know why I do this work I do, and why I create the home life I do. I know my why for everything.

Because of that, I've never worried about what somebody else will think when I put myself out there.

Fear of what other people think keeps many women stuck. Get and stay in touch with your mission and why you're doing this, and you'll stop caring so much about what other people think.

DUALITY DARE

Responsibility

Personal responsibility for our vision, our lives and our creation is Jessica's stand and how she views modern-day women. In some leadership pieces of training I've attended, one thing that changed my mindset at a very high level is understanding and embodying the concept of being 100% responsible 100% of the time.

When I am responsible, I can direct, guide, shift and lead my life. I get to take responsibility for my choices that lead to outcomes. Even when we don't like the outcome, we get to be responsible for it.

On the other side of the duality coin is when our choices lead to favorable outcomes. We also get to be 100% responsible for the choices that lead to outcomes we like.

We can't choose when to be responsible. We cannot be victims when things don't turn out favorably, and then be leaders and responsible when things do turn out favorably. You are leading your life from responsibility all the time, with every choice, decision, and circumstance, or you aren't.

This concept usually brings up resistance for people. If you're feeling triggered by being 100% responsible 100% of the time, I encourage you to go deeper.

What led to the outcome? Once you own those choices and understand your part in the outcome, you can take ownership. You can lead your life and make a different choice next time, by learning and applying the lesson.

Your Duality Dare is to go to the journal section and write down three adversities you get to be responsible for. That's three hardships, or three things you had to overcome, and how your choices during those times were your responsibility. Pick things you feel triggered thinking about being responsible for.

Use this prompt:

I am responsible for _____ because of this/these choices_____.

CHAPTER 5

STYLE
ROSE JUBB

Rose Jubb is a stylist and image consultant who works with personal clients virtually and developed an entire platform that helps women elevate their personal brand from the comfort of their own homes. Rose is a bestselling author, podcast host and recently launched her own makeover pilot called Closet Goals on Amazon Prime.

I grew up on a small hobby farm in Minnesota. My first real memory was fighting with my mom over which Minnie Mouse t-shirt I was wearing on my first day of kindergarten. After days of fighting with Mom over what I'd wear, she never dressed me again.

My family worked hard, but we had to "garage sale" and thrift to even pass as fitting in. I had to imagine how I would transform a shirt into that cool Calvin Klein sweatshirt I wanted. That "I am going to make this work" experience developed many styling muscles I now use.

When I started, it was in art, not magazines or fashion school. I've always had an eye for art and design. I worked in several marketing departments doing that.

After marrying and then divorcing my high school sweetheart, I moved across the country and away from everything I knew to start fresh. I even returned to school for psychology. At the time, it really lit my fire.

I got my master's degree, became a counselor, and then had my son and burn out. I was working in mental health, domestic violence, and homelessness. I knew I wanted to help women, but I also knew I wanted to be home for my son.

Meanwhile, this entire time I'd been styling friends and family members, thinking that could never be a career.

Eventually, somebody insisted on paying me to style them. As soon as I said yes to that, it was clients, clients, clients.

HOW DO YOU DEFINE A MODERN WOMAN?

The word balance comes to mind--or rather, the illusion of balance. Sometimes you can get so caught up in taking care of everybody else that you forget about yourself.

When you're an in demand modern woman, it's hard sometimes to explain to people what it's like, especially to partners and friends who aren't entrepreneurial or don't have high visibility careers or businesses. It's hard to explain what we do and why it's complicated.

Recently I explored how generations change and base their opinions on what's going on around them.

For people in their 20s, 30s, 40s, maybe even 50s, it's a stressful time. You may be taking care of little ones while you're worrying about your parents.

We also have all the pings, all the messages, the news--many things-- coming at us.

Other generations didn't have all this information to worry about and stress over. It comes with a lot of opportunities, as well, which is so wonderful. We can connect with people locally but also around the world. There's a silver lining, but it's still a lot to take on, especially on your own.

IN WHAT AREAS OF YOUR LIFE HAVE YOU STEPPED OUT OF CULTURAL NORMS, DEFIED THEM, OR GONE AGAINST THEM? AND IN THOSE AREAS OF YOUR LIFE WHERE YOU'VE DONE THAT, HAVE YOU EXPERIENCED ANY SHAME OR GUILT, EITHER EXTERNAL OR INTERNAL? IF SO, HOW DID YOU MANAGE THAT?

My passion for styling people, helping them feel amazing, and feeling like themselves wasn't a career I came from. By just doing that, I'm pushing boundaries.

It also pushed boundaries when I got divorced, moved across the country to live in a houseful of ladies I met on Craigslist, and to go back to school in my mid-twenties.

Having my passion be my career is also not the norm. For years I wanted to be that stylist, but I wouldn't even admit it. I feared failure and what people would think.

Finally, I've learned that it's not a good idea if I'm deciding out of desperation. It's good to wait a little bit. But if I'm making it because it feels right, it feels good, then it's something that's going to propel me forward.

I'd rather do it and fail at it, and learn from it, than not do it and wonder what would have happened.

Besides, every time I've decided based on what I love and need, instead of what everybody expected me to do, I got positive feedback internally instead of externally.

It was jet fuel compared to gasoline. It was that internal love of self and taking action inspired by that, which propelled me forward to keep making decisions that were for me instead of everyone else.

HOW DO YOU TAP INTO YOUR DIVINE FEMININE AND WILD SIDE EACH DAY?

Between my husband, my son, and even my dog, I'm surrounded by testosterone in my house. That's why having a circle of women I really trust, and who see the best in me, don't need things from me, and can serve as my sounding board, is so important.

I love my family, but they need things from me, and I need things from them. When you're in that dynamic with someone, it skews their opinions. Sometimes when people who love you want you to be safe, they also want you to be small. They worry when you do things that feel scary.

I also use clothes and makeup to feel feminine. I don't mean the pink and ruffles and lace kind of feminine. I mean feminine where you're in touch with your intuition and trusting yourself.

That's all about your identity, and we put on our identity every day. We have it internally. Everybody has a personal style; it's just a matter of whether or not you're truly embodying it.

When you get clear about who you are, and guide yourself towards your actual personal style that makes you feel the most confident, to me, that is super feminine.

Even when it doesn't quite align with what society thinks is feminine, you'll feel confident and like yourself, and that's what matters most. Confidence is better than compliments.

DUALITY DARE

Style

There was a time I thought I didn't have a style. After years of owning gyms and being a personal trainer, my style consisted of black leggings and a lululemon hoodie. I never explored the side of myself that could be stylish. In hindsight, maybe I didn't feel worthy of going and buying clothes for myself, or investigating what made me feel good, confident and sexy.

I didn't take the time to discover my style, and maybe you haven't either. Now in my 40s, and in a different season of my life and personal identity, I've realized I exude the most confidence when I feel like me, and when I dress like myself and for myself.

When I dress like the highest version of myself, when I wear bold earrings and my signature bright purple lipstick, it gives me a powerful sense of femininity and sensuality.

I look at style as a form of self-care--as a way to pull out your identity and confidence, to show the world who you are, and to show up transparently and in vulnerability.

For this Duality Dare, ask yourself how to step into the highest version of yourself using your personal style. Go into your closet today and put on clothes that make you feel your best.

Maybe it's just one item to start, or maybe it's that scarf you've been dying to wear, but it's a little bit too bold, so you keep putting it back in the drawer.

Maybe it's that Bolero hat that's been calling your name that you really want to wear because it feels so good when you have it on, but your logical mind keeps talking you out of it because, "Who do you think you are wearing a hat?!"

Maybe you just start with a new lipstick shade, or that sexy pair of panties that have been sitting in your lingerie drawer unseen for a decade.

Whatever it is, try something new today and be curious about your own identity and style. What makes you feel like your most feminine, confident, powerful self?

CHAPTER 6

QUEEN
PIRIE JONES GROSSMAN

Pirie Jones Grossman is a life empowerment coach, TEDx speaker, best selling author, and podcast host of Own Your Throne podcast. She's shared the stage with thought leaders like His Holiness, the Dalai Lama, Deepak Chopra, Marianne Williamson, and many more.

I was raised by a schizophrenic mother who ended up in a mental institution. I had a lot of issues around self-worth and self-love. When I was in LA working on television, people would see me working and think, "Oh, my God, that girl's got it so together."

I didn't. I was a big pretender because I was the scared little girl who just wanted to be loved on the inside.

I didn't learn how to truly love and empower myself until I was in my 50s. It took many inner journeys.

One thing that really helped me was when I started healing what I call "the mother wound," with some wonderful work by Bethany Webster. I just got in there, forgave my mom, and forgave myself.

As women, we like to share and chat and just say, "Oh, my God, this is what happened to me." And it came out of a lot of vulnerabilities.

That was what brought me into coaching. I wanted to see other women heal like I did. I knew there were tools and techniques out there where they could.

Nothing brings me more joy than to see a woman transform and fall in love with herself, and truly be in her divine feminine. That's my purpose, to help women do that.

HOW DO YOU DEFINE A MODERN WOMAN?

A modern woman is one who's healed and made the inner journey. She has self-esteem, is independent and fierce, and doesn't put her life up for vote. Confidence comes from within.

In *Discovering the Inner Mother*, author Bethany Webster says we live in a society that tells mothers to be loving all the time and care for others. A good mother puts her needs last and serves the family first. But if we don't do the individual work and heal those wounds, the world will lose out on empowered women in their divine feminine.

Society says we're the nurturers. That's true, but it's not all we are. I'm also a business owner, coach, girlfriend, and friend.

Some women think their power comes from their masculinity. When I worked in business, I was in my masculine mode, and my personal life was falling apart. I've been married and divorced four times because I gave my power away.

My mother wound is a big part of why. My mom showed very conditional love and was jealous. When I healed that wound, my business and personal life integrated. My masculine and feminine integrated into the full-on feminine divine.

I was very close to my dad, so I loved and trusted men. I did not trust women. I competed against them in beauty pageants and for work in Hollywood.

Now I love women. The power in the girl tribe is amazing. I could still have my lift from men, but I'm not going to give my power away anymore.

IN WHAT AREAS OF YOUR LIFE HAVE YOU STEPPED OUT OF CULTURAL NORMS, DEFIED THEM, OR GONE AGAINST THEM? AND IN THOSE AREAS OF YOUR LIFE WHERE YOU'VE DONE THAT, HAVE YOU EXPERIENCED ANY SHAME OR GUILT, EITHER EXTERNAL OR INTERNAL? IF SO, HOW DID YOU MANAGE THAT?

I had the hardest time permitting myself to love myself. I am a rule breaker in business and never really cared what society thought, but I had a hard time doing it personally. When I was trying to have kids in my 30s, the male doctors said, "Your eggs are too old. Why didn't you do this earlier if you really wanted a child?"

Finally, I met a doctor who checked me out and said it didn't matter how old you are. I had my children at 44 and 46.

A modern day woman doesn't give her health to somebody else. Become your own medical advocate, ask questions, use your voice. You deserve to feel fabulous.

I definitely went against the grain of the patriarch by listening more to my intuition. The more I shared my voice, the more confident I got, and the more I healed. Now breaking glass ceilings is really easy for me. When someone tells me, "Well, you can't really do that," it's a green light to do it.

Whenever I get into that mode of not knowing, and my little girl is acting up, I talk with her. I believe everyone has all the answers inside of them. Sometimes we get clouded by the wounded little girl, teenager, or mother.

Solve this by getting into your Queen energy. Find a chair in your home, in a sacred space, and make it a throne. Get yourself a crown. Then sit on your throne, put the tiara on, and say, "What would the Queen do?"

HOW DO YOU TAP INTO YOUR DIVINE FEMININE AND WILD SIDE EACH DAY?

I go on trips with girlfriends, kiss my boyfriend, and have fantasy things I do. I like to play different roles. I like to spoil myself and go to the spa. I make sure any emotional toxins I have inside are removed.

Every morning I say this prayer: "God, just use me in any way that I can be used as a vessel for your good and the highest good of all."

I also know when to say no. If I'm overextending myself, I look at what brings me joy. Joy keeps you in the light where you can give more to your family and friends.

We've got to get out of this notion that speaking up is wrong. No, it's not. It's powerful. If you can't do it yourself, find that chair, go get the crown, put it on, and speak like the Queen.

Give yourself permission to explore all the different parts of you, including your dark and carnal sides. It's not wrong.

And take care of yourself. It's not selfish to meet your needs. Go within and ask yourself what you need to make yourself happy. Find your voice, and use it to ask for what you want.

You are more than you give yourself credit for.

DUALITY DARE

Queen

How do we become Queens of our own lives, and lead from a place of love, acceptance, and grace? How do we honor ourselves, and the shifts and adjustments we need as we navigate the seasons of our lives? Doing that is key to "Owning Your Throne", as Pirie would say.

The first step to standing in our power as Leaders of Our Lives is embodying our inner Queen, and validating our own inner wisdom and deep inherent value as women. We are life givers, creators, and QUEENS.

You may feel resistance to this Duality Dare. Declaring yourself a Queen may bring up worthiness issues. But if you can step into your own Queendom, aka the life you are creating, and embody that kind of responsibility and ownership of your life's path, you are well on your way to creating a life that you love--one that brings you joy, is authentic to you, and is aligned with your values.

Follow Pirie's advice and order a crown. Yes, right now! You might even have a toy crown in the house. Designate a chair in your house as your throne. Whenever you experience self-doubt, indecisiveness, or lack clarity...whenever you feel like you don't have authority or sovereignty in your life... here's what you do.

Sit in your throne with your crown on your head and ask, "What would the Queen do? How would the Queen act? How would the Queen speak? How would the Queen feel?"

CHAPTER 7

VALIDITY
EMILY LOUISE WILSON

Emily Louise Wilson is a health and fitness coach who focuses on helping people empower themselves through fitness and a plant-based lifestyle, so they can really thrive in their lives.

Health and fitness are my passion. A couple of years ago, I transitioned to a plant-based diet, and it's become one of my primary focuses. I saw how it transformed my life, and how I felt physically, mentally, and emotionally.

I also see the impact it has on people I know and on the planet. I'm super passionate about this lifestyle.

As far as the work that I do, I do one-on-one coaching with people looking to uplevel their health and fitness and who are interested in moving toward a plant-based lifestyle.

Not everyone I work with is 100% plant-based, and that's totally okay. I meet people where they're at.

What I find to be most important in my work is not so much the fitness plan or the nutrition plan.

What has become so apparent to me with all the women and men I've worked with is what's going on underneath the surface. As in, what's happening between our ears, and what's happening within our hearts. I've evolved my coaching and the work I do to incorporate more of that aspect.

Often when people come to work with me, they have different layers I help them uncover and break free from it as it relates to their beliefs--the stories they tell themselves about their health status, or their fitness status, or what they can and can't do in their lives.

The people who experience the most transformation do this inner work.

HOW DO YOU DEFINE A MODERN WOMAN?

The duality of being a modern woman is the ability to tap into my independence and be who I authentically am; and also maintain that authenticity with the people in my life.

Asking for support is not a part of my history. I take care of things for myself, and I expect other people to do the same. But I've come to recognize that quality in myself and that it doesn't always work.

In the last couple of years, I've shifted from focusing on my relationship dynamics with men to diving into my friendships with my girlfriends and the women in my family.

Part of making this leap involved recognizing that I did not trust women. I was adopted when I was an infant. I was removed from my birth mother, and didn't know how to process that. I internalized it as, "I don't trust women because I can't count on them to be there for me."

My ability to begin trusting women first came from my awareness that I didn't, and then playing with that idea of, is this even true?

There's a difference between what's true, and what's valid. That I felt I couldn't trust women is valid.

But it's not true. The truth is, I can trust women, because I had this other woman in my life, my mother, who took me as her own, which is one of the most beautiful things ever.

A modern woman can be independent and support herself including financially, but she can also be empowered with support from others.

IN WHAT AREAS OF YOUR LIFE HAVE YOU STEPPED OUT OF CULTURAL NORMS, DEFIED THEM, OR GONE AGAINST THEM? AND IN THOSE AREAS OF YOUR LIFE WHERE YOU'VE DONE THAT, HAVE YOU EXPERIENCED ANY SHAME OR GUILT, EITHER EXTERNAL OR INTERNAL? IF SO, HOW DID YOU MANAGE THAT?

My fitness for sure. For me, fitness is about moving my body because it makes me feel good. Weightlifting makes me feel like a badass.

I grew up doing gymnastics, and I had calloused hands and muscular shoulders. I would get feedback of, "That's not feminine," so I became self-conscious of my muscles and calloused hands. At the same time, I had so much fun training and moving my body. I didn't want to give it up.

I'm not willing to let that narrative of "women shouldn't be strong and muscular or lift heavy" change what I love. I love lifting weights, and I'm going to keep doing it, whether people accept it or not.

I also face self-consciousness around showing my body. How much do you reveal, how much do you not? If I show my body, am I going to make other women feel bad about theirs?

The flip side of that is, can I just feel good about my body for the sake of feeling good about my body? I've put a ton of work and effort into it. Why should I be ashamed of it or worry how other people will perceive it?

People are going to judge you, whether you post a picture of yourself in a bikini, or you post a picture of yourself not in a bikini. Stop making decisions based on what you think people will think.

You've been given one body in this lifetime. Give yourself some grace and enjoy what you have right now.

HOW DO YOU TAP INTO YOUR DIVINE FEMININE AND WILD SIDE EACH DAY?

Clothing and fashion. I love wearing clothes that make me feel beautiful, feel good on my skin, and accentuate parts of my physical frame that I find beautiful.

It's like playing dress-up, which I used to do all the time as a little girl. It's so much fun, and it makes me feel feminine.

I still get to bring out my wild side, but I will say I love being in nature. I have this duality where I like being clean, but I also love certain things that don't qualify as "clean" by some standards, like walking around barefoot, or being in the ocean and the sand, and not worrying about what gets all over me.

Being in nature allows me to tap into that wild side because I feel connected to the earth.

The other thing I would say brings out my wild side is music: music and dancing. I love to dance. And usually, I don't care what I look like, or if people see me.

I also took off three months to live in the Caribbean. Definitely living on the wild side there!

DUALITY DARE

Validity

There is a difference. Where can you find a belief that is not serving you between what is valid and what is true?

Your Duality Dare is about finding the blind spots in the story you might have told yourself regarding what is a valid concept or belief and what is actually the truth.

After you identify the disconnect between what is valid and true, can you extract evidence that the belief could be untrue?

For example, as Emily discusses, it's valid that she doesn't trust women because she's had some breakdowns in her life and a disconnect within the Sisterhood, but is it true that women can't be trusted? No, of course not.

Where can we logically anchor to that truth? Where can we extract evidence that she can trust women?

Go back in your history and extract evidence of truth. Your belief is valid. If it's not serving you, create evidence in your history to counter that belief. For example, if you feel that you cannot trust women, how can you find evidence in your history of when you could trust women? Identify a specific example.

If you absolutely cannot find your own evidence of trust, where can you find it from an example of a strong Sisterhood with other women, where women trusting other women is modeled.

It's not enough to just think about this. Turn to the journal at the end of the book and dive in!

CHAPTER 8

SEXUALITY
KARI MISCHELL

Kari Mischell is a Certified Body Connection Coach, and a Mind Body Wellness Practitioner who specializes in emotional releases.

I had an eating disorder for twelve years, plus body dysmorphia and exercise addiction. All the pain from everything I experienced over those twelve years created the opportunity for my passion and my purpose.

So did those experiences of disconnection from my own body. I experienced deep disconnection and shame around my sexuality, so I began a beautiful process of yearning for it--for the connection and a healthy relationship with my sexuality and femininity.

Once I figured out how to truly claim and own those parts of me, I thought, "Oh my gosh, I have to share this with the world!" Since then, my coaching program has morphed and blossomed into what it is now.

What's beautiful is that I'm continually growing, and so is my business. As I continue to dive deeper into my connection, and my intimacy with myself, everything will continually change and evolve.

I love where it's at now, and I'm so excited about where it's going.

HOW DO YOU DEFINE A MODERN WOMAN?

It's embodying your divine feminine in a very bold way. A lot of times, when we think of being in the feminine, we associate it with less-than. We think we're going to be weaker, and not valued or respected.

The way we do that is not with a "screw men" mindset. A modern woman respects and loves the masculine and also fully owns her divine feminine. She feels safe in her flow, in her sensuality, in her sexuality, and in her ability to be able to receive and create.

She feels safe in her emotions, and she expresses them daily. Women are emotional beings. That is a gift we get to enjoy.

We're also very sexual. I want to clarify what is sex and what is sexuality, because there's much incorrect programming around it. When a woman is truly able to embody her pleasure and her creative flow, and she's receiving and creating, that's when she's manifesting. There is no limit to what you can create while in your divine feminine flow.

Being in that flow not about the doing. I'm not saying you just sit on your meditation pillow and wait for your business to create itself. I'm saying you get into the space of flow and trust that your intuition will guide you. When it does, you take inspired action.

When you're in that space, nothing feels like "doing." You're just flowing with what's being created, as if you're riding a wave. I'm creating so much more with my business now being in my feminine flow.

IN WHAT AREAS OF YOUR LIFE HAVE YOU STEPPED OUT OF CULTURAL NORMS, DEFIED THEM, OR GONE AGAINST THEM? AND IN THOSE AREAS OF YOUR LIFE WHERE YOU'VE DONE THAT, HAVE YOU EXPERIENCED ANY SHAME OR GUILT, EITHER EXTERNAL OR INTERNAL? IF SO, HOW DID YOU MANAGE THAT?

There's a lot of shame around sex, but the feminine's power is in her sexual energy. For sex to take place, a receiving and a giving both have to happen. Sex creates life in a woman's body, and a woman births that creation.

That energy of giving, receiving, and creating is not limited to the act of sex. When we're in that energy, we're in the energy of creation and manifestation.

When we pinch off that energy, we feel like we need to hustle and work hard, and that's why we stop feeling alive.

These days, a lot of sexual energy is devoted to feeding our carnal desires, and we're not including our heart. We're not including our connection to the divine. But when we include all those things, and we're in that energy, whether we're in the act of lovemaking or we're creating content for our business, magic happens.

Sensuality has a bad rap, too. Sensuality is simply the engagement of your five senses. Even just putting your lotion on can be a sensual experience, meaning you're including all your senses. And when you're doing that, you're slowing down and being present, and then you're in your flow. When you can get into your flow, inspiration and creative energy come easily.

We really have to question these programs we have around sexuality and sensuality. When we decided that sexuality is just in the bedroom, and when we're being provocative, we're missing the whole beauty and the power of what that energy truly is.

HOW DO YOU TAP INTO YOUR DIVINE FEMININE AND WILD SIDE EACH DAY?

My biggest secret to getting into my divine feminine flow is playing, because the feminine is playful. She's all about flirting, playing, having fun and being light. We're programmed to believe that once we turn 18, we need to be serious and boring. That makes it hard to access your divine feminine flow.

Another thing I often do during my meditation, is sing. Our pussy is made of the same tissue as our throat, so as I activate my throat with singing, I'm also activating my pussy, which puts me into that creative energy.

I'll also get out my hula hoop or do some roller skating, as I did as a little girl.

I naturally have a good chunk of masculine in me, which for a long time was really dominant. It's really easy for me to move into that once I know what action I need to take. Inspiration comes through. Then I move into my masculine energy to execute it.

When I do that, I have to remind myself that I don't have to hustle. I'll tell myself, "Just open and receive, Kari, just open and receive."

About 20% of women are actually in their masculine, but the other 80% thrive in their feminine. Yet society-wide, it's flipped. Eighty percent of women are in their masculine when they really should be thriving in their feminine.

It's not a surprise. We've been programmed that way. Now we're waking up to the fact it's just not serving anybody--us or the masculine.

DUALITY DARE

Sexuality

Sex can be play. Sex is pleasure. We get to step into our desires.

The first way to reconnect with our sexual pleasure is to explore pleasure through play. This is the gateway to being fully present with your divine feminine.

For so long so many of us women have been led to believe that anything that gives us pleasure through sexuality or sensuality is wrong or bad, and we should be ashamed of it.

I would like to unravel that narrative. I want to bring back the connection to our bodies without shame, the connection to pleasure without shame, the connection to our desire without shame. It starts with being explorative and curious about what pleasures us in non-sexual ways, so we can begin to remember how to create pleasure with our sensuality and sexuality. How can we bring more sensuality into our daily lives?

For your Duality Dare, I'm asking you to step out of your comfort zone and begin to play again. Play is the first step to getting us connected with pleasure.

What can you do today to bring yourself into a playful way of being? What can you do today that actually brings you joy, and takes you back to that little girl who played all day, free of shame or guilt? What did she enjoy? What brought her pleasure? Was it the monkey bars? Cartwheels? Dancing, singing, drawing, or riding her bike all over town with her friends?

Take ten minutes to rediscover that part of you that might be forgotten. Look beyond the part of you that may have become rigid and doesn't allow time for fun, play, or sensual release.

Sensuality is all about experiencing our senses, as Kari says in her interview. How can you experience play through your senses today?

CHAPTER 9

UNITY
BARBARA KAMBA-NYATHI

Barbara Kamba-Nyathi, who hails from Zimbabwe, is a lifestyle and wellness coach, bestselling author, TEDx motivational and inspirational speaker, and psychotherapist. Barbara is also the founder and CEO of Bold Dialogue magazine, where she helps empower women through emotional release to step into their genius.

My journey has been nothing short of miraculous. In 2009, I was diagnosed with stage three cervical cancer, which saved my life, because it led to the discovery, a few months later, of stage four endometrial cancer.

The cancer diagnosis helped me be kinder to myself and understand myself. It helps me remember everyone may be going through something they may not be sharing. But everyone goes through something, and we need to learn to be compassionate.

For a while, I completely lost my ability to hear, and during that time, I learned to listen with more than my ears. I'd watch their facial expressions and observe how they were dressed, because that also communicated how they were feeling.

I also got to engage my sixth sense--my intuition--and develop my Third Eye, because I got to observe people, not just from a physical perspective, but in a more spiritual way that's beyond just what someone appears to be.

Another pivotal part of my journey was enduring serial cheating in my marriage. My ex was turning toward younger girls. The first time I discovered it, I wanted to divorce him. I phoned a friend who's a judge and told her. She said no, don't divorce him. Stay and heal yourself in that marriage. After you've healed, if you still want to divorce, then divorce.

Learning to heal in the eye of the storm like that was a rocky journey. It helped me realize that life's not always about where you want to go. It's about the journey. It's like being refined. That's the best way to describe it.

HOW DO YOU DEFINE A MODERN WOMAN?

For me, it's a woman who knows what she wants, and doesn't apologize for wanting it and going after it. It's important to be a woman who stands in her truth, no matter what.

That can include being a woman who will walk out of something, any relationship, regardless of the nature of the relationship, when it's not helping her.

Yet she also finds her inner healing--her emotional footing, if you will--before stepping out. Sometimes we're so hurt, we're limping. We want to jump out, right out. What we don't know is that we're going to be hurt even more if we jump without making sure we have our "emotional crutches," or that we're already healing from our pain.

To do that, we can get help, both in therapy and by belonging to a tribe—a sisterhood. Nobody understands a human like your fellow human.

We may not be on the exact same journey, but we have that deep connection inside of us that will make me feel for you, whatever you're going through.

With some friends of mine, if one of us was hurting, someone else would buy ice cream, go to the friend, sit on the floor, or cushions on the carpet, and eat ice cream. If she wants to talk, she will talk. If she doesn't, we just eat ice cream. When done, we hug each other and tell each other we love each other.

You need those close friends, those close sisters who will hold you up, and who will sit down with you.

IN WHAT AREAS OF YOUR LIFE HAVE YOU STEPPED OUT OF CULTURAL NORMS, DEFIED THEM, OR GONE AGAINST THEM? AND IN THOSE AREAS OF YOUR LIFE WHERE YOU'VE DONE THAT, HAVE YOU EXPERIENCED ANY SHAME OR GUILT, EITHER EXTERNAL OR INTERNAL? IF SO, HOW DID YOU MANAGE THAT?

My childhood prepared me for this. I was born with autoimmune disease, so I've always been different. In primary school, I was treated for arthritis.

I'm a girl from Africa, where the sun is in abundance, yet because of my autoimmune disease and treatments, I shed off skin when I would step in the sun. It was painful. Imagine having to learn that you don't play in the sun, while living in an area where the sun is abundant.

All that prepared me to be seen and treated differently. I learned to embrace my differences, my uniqueness, and just celebrate it, no matter what other people think of me.

People talk, of course. The ones who don't understand say the most. Even so, I celebrate my uniqueness.

In African society, a woman's identity is strongly linked to her children. There comes the point, at a certain age, where instead of being addressed by your first name, you're addressed as a mother of "your child's name."

But I cannot procreate. I have no children of my own. I've accepted that and focus on being the best auntie I can be.

Another part of my culture I've defied is the idea that you need a man to take care of you. I work for myself, and care for myself.

There's also a lot of judgement about a woman exploring her sexuality, especially when she's not married. I am not shy about exploring my sexuality.

HOW DO YOU TAP INTO YOUR DIVINE FEMININE AND WILD SIDE EACH DAY?

For me, it's about meditation. When I tap into everything, I focus on what I want to achieve and where I want to go. Then I bring it together.

It's also about understanding that I may be doing everything for myself, but my source that sustains me is the backbone. It gives me the shape I want to achieve. Plus it gives me the liberty to tap into my masculine self and not lose the feminine unity in me.

It's also understanding that I am energy meant to align with other energies. There's a saying that I love that says, "a person is a person because of other people." It puts everything into perspective.

It doesn't matter where we're coming from. It's about the story--the mosaic we're building from our brokenness, that's speaking to each of us.

This mosaic runs deeper than the physical sisterhood. It's a spiritual sisterhood. It's why we understand each other. It's why we can step into our different journeys, and despite the differences in our struggles, we realize you are holding a light for me at the end of the tunnel, and I'm also holding a light for you.

I'm a lifestyle and wellness coach, and I believe in holistic living. When you are okay emotionally, spiritually, and physically--once those parts are connected--you approach everything else you do from that healed, whole place. You also attract people into your life who complement you.

DUALITY DARE

Unity

How can we allow the mosaic of your Brokenness to create unity and healing?

I used to think all of my broken pieces would never allow me to amount to anything. I used to think that my Brokenness made me vulnerable, weak and insignificant; that the dark, shadowy places I hid from, ignored, and brushed underneath the rug would never allow me to create anything beautiful (especially as beautiful as a bright, colorful mosaic).

I discovered that each time I healed one of those broken pieces and healed a part of myself, I also healed the collective. When we heal ourselves, we give permission for other women to heal and become a ripple in the consciousness of the Sisterhood.

Your Duality Dare is to allow yourself to look at your "broken" pieces as the gateway to co-creating a beautiful, unified mosaic. What parts of you can you allow to be seen so they can heal? Where is the darkness in your past and in your subconscious that makes you feel unworthy, insignificant or broken?

Identify at least one of these "broken" pieces and forgive yourself. Use the journal portion of this book to write down this "broken" piece. Write down one way you can accept and/or forgive yourself. Then write down one way this piece of your unique mosaic actually fits perfectly in the masterpiece of your life. Write down how this brokenness shaped the design of the mosaic and your life.

Then consider it's possible that you're not broken at all, and each individual piece is part of the co-created mosaic unifying millions of other "broken" pieces, all designed to illuminate, reflect, and bring brilliance, radiance, and healing into the world.

Without the dark and light polarity, the birthing of the universal mosaic that can heal the collective would never be unearthed. The healing of one is the healing of many.

BEAUTY
TOBEY ANN TERRY

Tobey Ann Terry is a best-selling author and beauty and empowerment coach. A beauty industry leader for over 25 years, Tobey is the founder and creator of Naked Soul Beauty organic skincare line.

The beauty industry is something I just dropped into. I wasn't thinking about it during my childhood or high school years, though all my favorite classes were art and photography in high school.

Then, one day I woke up, and I said, "I want to go to beauty school."

I respected my hairstylist, and my mom respected all the beauty pros in her life. I knew they made great money, and they made their own hours. It just felt really great

From there, my business elevated into different revenue streams, and into multiple other businesses I've started. All are either completely in line with the beauty industry or have a common thread with it.

I started when I was nineteen. It's been a fun journey!

I'm all about the fun, even within my coaching. Not everything we do in life is fun, but when it comes to the things you choose in or the way you approach things, infuse as much fun as you can.

I also help women in business get on camera with confidence, and unite that inner and outer beauty, so you can show up and deliver with magic and shine.

HOW DO YOU DEFINE A MODERN WOMAN?

Doing what you want, when you want to. Doing what lights you up, what makes you feel the most passion in your life, and owning it.

If that's your work, go all in. A modern woman is not asking for permission and not apologizing. She's feeling the stumbles, feeling the pain, feeling the failures and the mistakes, then owning it, getting up, and moving on.

It doesn't have to be the traditional things women have done for years. I love talking about women in the 1950s because they were the pioneers of self-care. They were not sitting around meditating and journaling. They went to the salon and drank martinis.

Even if you're a 50s housewife, you can still put on high heels, lipstick, and drink a martini at four o'clock.

The point is, what lights you up? Is it meditation, journaling, and going within? Or more passion, or more growth in your career? What feels good in your heart?

IN WHAT AREAS OF YOUR LIFE HAVE YOU STEPPED OUT OF CULTURAL NORMS, DEFIED THEM, OR GONE AGAINST THEM? AND IN THOSE AREAS OF YOUR LIFE WHERE YOU'VE DONE THAT, HAVE YOU EXPERIENCED ANY SHAME OR GUILT, EITHER EXTERNAL OR INTERNAL? IF SO, HOW DID YOU MANAGE THAT?

For one, I'm a mom, but I'm not as wrapped up in the day-to-day of motherhood and getting overwhelmed by it as a lot of moms are. When I'm with my twins, I'm _with_ my twins. They see me, they love me, we do things together. But you're not going to see me at every drop off and pick up, every play date and party, or every sporting event.

I give my children my all, but I don't give them all my time, and I'm okay with that. I'm striving for something bigger and greater, so I can support them and love them in ways that are amazing for the rest of their lives.

For another, when I got divorced, I divorced a man that everybody loved, including me. We were best friends and had a lot in common. But I reached a point where I wanted to do life with someone who really wanted to grow within themselves. I'd evolved, and he wasn't evolving in a way that I still wanted to be married to.

As far as the outside world was concerned, there was no reason for me to file for divorce, so a lot of guilt and shame came at me from all different angles, especially for "breaking up the family." I had my own guilt over it, too, because he didn't do anything wrong.

I got into another relationship for a while, and it was great, but I left it behind because I realized I just wanted to be with my kids, and my business, and with me. I don't need to be attached to anyone.

HOW DO YOU TAP INTO YOUR DIVINE FEMININE AND WILD SIDE EACH DAY?

When my divorce was happening, I did anything and everything I could get my hands on in terms of spiritual work. I cried all the time. I prayed. You name it.

And then I united that with the outer beauty aspect. When I didn't have my kids, I'd go have fun. I'd go out with my friends.

Your life doesn't have to be cookie cutter. It doesn't have to be the way people around us are doing it.

My ex and I love each other. We're both good people. Not every divorced couple has the bond we have, or can live the way we're living.

61

We are doing this for our kids, but we're doing it for ourselves, too. I don't want to go back to the whole idea of giving up everything for your kids. That's not what I'm saying by saying we do this partly for our kids.

I'm saying that when you do something for your kids and it builds up you, and your values and your character and your traits and your story--the core of who you are--that's the modern woman.

DUALITY DARE

Beauty

The beauty in the bravery of non-conformity is real. The beauty of being able to step into your authenticity and shed the conditioning of cultural norms...the beauty of truly living in alignment with your own values and Truth...this is the beauty that Tobey speaks about in her interview.

To be non-conforming is brave. I believe that what Tobey is describing is the ability to love boldly and with bravery, and let go of the fear of what we've been conditioned to believe is our path.

Tobey shares that to unify our external and internal beauty, we have to be authentic. We have to be brave enough to live in nonconformity and in alignment with our truth.

This Duality Dare is about unearthing your bravery and stepping into nonconformity. What area(s) of your life can you push the envelope into what feels true for you, but might be scary to unravel? What area of your life are you conditioned to believe you must choose, but your heart and soul and intuition are nudging you to take a different path?

Go to the journal section and write down one way you've conformed, but you know is not in alignment with your Truth. Then commit to taking the next best behavior to break the conformity and act into your Truth by stepping through the cultural conditioning.

CHAPTER 11

MOM-GUILT
ARIANNA BRADFORD

Arianna Bradford is a parent, advocate, speaker, activist, and author of Shame On You: Big Truth From A Bad Mom.

Originally I was a photographer, and took pictures of parents, families, seniors--the usual photographer stuff. In April of 2016 I had my second child, and that's when it clicked that there's this unrealistic expectation of parents--especially mothers--to take on everything emotionally, physically, and mentally.

So, I started something called the NYAM Project (Not Your Average Mom), with the point of showing that there's no such thing as "just a mom." Meaning, there's no such thing as a woman with no history and background, who's not a person underneath the parent.

As I started talking on Instagram about my personal experiences and thoughts, it resonated with many people. It showed me that my message needed to be tweaked.

I realized that before I could start talking to people outside the realm of parenthood, I had to start talking to parents. We were still judging ourselves and each other, and if we can't come together to understand that parenthood is a different experience for everybody, we can't get other people to understand it, either.

That's why I say I'm a parent advocate. I advocate for parents to parent themselves just as much as they parent their kids, because we often forget to do that.

It's become a real passion of mine to help people understand that parenting is not what we're being told it is; it _is_ what we're experiencing every day.

HOW DO YOU DEFINE A MODERN WOMAN?

I think it's under construction right now, which is great. The old definition was so full of contradictions that it was impossible to achieve.

You have to speak softly. Yet you have to have endless energy to take care of your children, meet your family's needs, and make sure you work.

But you also have to work as if you don't have children, and have children as if you don't work. You're supposed to be fit, but you're also supposed to be cool enough to eat pizza and chips and cookies and ice cream whenever your kids want. You have to be everything. It's too much.

Not everyone gets it yet. There's still plenty of women out there who are very dedicated to people-pleasing.

Case in point: In a weird tweet of mine a while back, I joked about the second day of your period, and how you have to do "that waddle" to get to the toilet when you first wake up in the morning.

I also got one very bizarre response to that tweet from a woman who said, "I just want all men to know that we don't all flow like that."

I remember thinking, "Why do men need to know how you flow? Or how you don't? Why are you so worried about pleasing people with your period flow?"

Even though many people are still stuck in an outdated way, I feel we're starting to grow out of it and recognize that being a woman is about being a person, not being the stereotype.

IN WHAT AREAS OF YOUR LIFE HAVE YOU STEPPED OUT OF CULTURAL NORMS, DEFIED THEM, OR GONE AGAINST THEM? AND IN THOSE AREAS OF YOUR LIFE WHERE YOU'VE DONE THAT, HAVE YOU EXPERIENCED ANY SHAME OR GUILT, EITHER EXTERNAL OR INTERNAL? IF SO, HOW DID YOU MANAGE THAT?

Being a black woman in America has rebelliousness to it, just because there are lots of assumptions people make about me.

I also developed rebelliousness by being a musician, which helped me as a parent. I "rebelliously" started acknowledging when I was annoyed, or angry, or happy because when I ignore how I feel, I'm not showing my children or myself who I am.

Acknowledging and showing how I feel taught my kids how to admit when they're angry. It also showed them not to screw with me, which taught them how to take care of themselves. Unexpectedly, it also taught my husband how to take care of himself.

I'm even honest about when I don't enjoy parenting, which happens. Most people are terrified to talk about that because other people get so upset.

But when we're not allowed to talk about things, they fester. People need to understand it's okay, and it can be done without ruining your child.

It's also okay if you feel guilty. I don't tell people not to feel guilty because it's impossible. It's a chemical reaction in your brain.

I see guilt as a warning system, like a smoke alarm. When your smoke alarm goes off, you don't automatically call 911. You check to see what's going on. If there is no smoke, you turn off the alarm.

That's what you do when feeling guilty. Don't give into the guilt. Just acknowledge, analyze, and decide your following action.

All this needs to be the norm. Moms need to focus themselves, too.

HOW DO YOU TAP INTO YOUR DIVINE FEMININE AND WILD SIDE EACH DAY?

I regularly struggle with feeling feminine. I've been told I have a "masculine energy." Do people who say that mean I have a loud mouth, and I don't back down on some things? I don't know why that's masculine, necessarily.

Things that help me feel powerful or feminine tend to come more from matching my outside to my inside. For example, I wash my hair, brush out the curls, put on earrings, and put on makeup. I wear clothes that make me feel powerful.

When I know inside that I'm the person looking great on the outside, it tends to make me feel stronger.

As for being wild, I don't know how to be any other way. It's funny. When I was a kid, I was one of those people with no filter between her brain and her mouth. Whatever I thought, I said.

Back then, I struggled with that. I remember thinking people would like me more in high school if I was quiet, less wild, less in your face.

Since then, I've embraced it. It's who I am. I am the one in my group of friends who busts out with a joke everyone laughs at, but also asks, "Oh, why did you take it there?"

There are times when it is okay to be the whirlwind. People are gonna love you for it regardless. Those are the people you're speaking to, not the people who don't love you for it.

DUALITY DARE

Mom-guilt

Parenting is no joke. As women, we receive a lot of pressure to parent correctly, do everything right, and present ourselves handling it all and being it all for our children no matter what. It's almost like we get a Mom of the Year award if we self-deprecate or deprive ourselves of basic self-care.

I also find that women do not talk about the hard parts of motherhood. Personally, I'm not the kind of mom that laid on the floor with my daughter playing Barbies. I didn't love singing nursery rhymes. I just wasn't that kind of mom. I felt guilty for it and ashamed that I didn't enjoy the things other moms gushed about.

I tried, and I tried, and I tried some more, but I never really felt connected to it. All the other moms seemed to have it all figured out, and I felt like it was a victory to have my daughter dressed in clean clothes with a banana in hand and on time for preschool. Meanwhile, other moms showed up carrying lattes and perfectly packed lunches with kids whose hair was actually combed. I could not relate.

The way I love my daughter and show up for her is my business, and I get to love and support her without guilt or shame or expectations.

So do you. The way you show up for your children, your nieces, your nephews, the children and young people in your life that you nurture and mentor doesn't have to look a certain way. It just needs one element--to come from a place of love. In our culture, I believe we forgot this in the striving for parent perfection. It's a journey, and we're going to get it wrong, but we're also going to get it right. It's not always going to be easy, it's not always going to flow, and sometimes we're going to want to pull our hair out.

I do know that however you decide to parent your children, this should not be up for judgment or pull you deep into the mom guilt trap. You know your children best, and you know yourself best.

I want this Duality Dare to open up your idea of what being a good parent really is. What if you experimented with your parenting style and did the opposite of everything that you typically do with your children?

What if you allowed them not to eat their vegetables? What if you allowed them to play outside a little bit past dinner time? What if you allowed them more freedom than you typically do?

What if your children did wear mismatched clothes? What if their lunch isn't gluten-free? What if you decided not to take your kids to that after-school activity? What if you played outside the boundaries of "perfect parenting," as per our current cultural narrative, and what if you could create evidence that no one was going to call the bad parent police?

I dare you to let go of the perfect parent narrative and explore the boundaries of your inner knowing. What norms or rules can you break today with your children? Identify one and let it flow!

CHAPTER 12

BREADWINNER
CHRISTA NICHOLS

Christa Nichols is an Iowa farm wife turned high ticket sales copywriter for seven and eight figure entrepreneurs. Christa is super passionate about encouraging other women to dig deep and discover what they didn't know they were capable of, and take action to accomplish their big dreams.

I grew up in a conservative home. My dad is a farmer, and my mom stayed home and took care of us kids. She also had a little side business, but she never had a career.

Growing up, knowing how safe and idyllic my childhood was, I wanted that for my kids.

I live in the middle of Iowa cornfields, literally. My husband and I have two teenagers, and we utilize a combination of homeschool and dual enrollment, which means we're in and out of school all the time. We're total bleacher parents!

My husband and I both work from home, and we both have businesses. He's also the project manager in my business, in addition to managing another business. We're all up in the entrepreneurial space.

We love hanging out on the farm playing games, lifting weights, and being outside (when it's not negative 25 degrees). We live life with whomever God puts in our path.

HOW DO YOU DEFINE A MODERN WOMAN?

It's also a woman who takes charge of her life, discovers what she's good at and passionate about, and uses it to serve other people.

Taking charge of your life doesn't mean you have to clash with everyone. That may happen, but it doesn't have to.

For me, my husband's been one of my biggest supporters. I never wanted to be the breadwinner, and I didn't think I was capable of it.

After my husband's injuries left us with no choice but to be the breadwinner, I discovered I was capable of so much more than I thought. A big part of that is because he believed in me...in us...and that we could do this.

Leaning on the belief of others is a huge part of how I made it this far. I joined a mastermind when we couldn't afford it, and it surrounded me with people who saw the potential of what could be. It became a network of people who believed when I couldn't. The coach in that program believed in me way before I did.

Now we have people who help us so that my husband can have more of his time. But the support of my network and my family has been huge.

A modern woman can discover and operate in her zone of genius without sacrificing relationships with the people she loves. And she can lean on the belief of others while she learns to believe in herself.

IN WHAT AREAS OF YOUR LIFE HAVE YOU STEPPED OUT OF CULTURAL NORMS, DEFIED THEM, OR GONE AGAINST THEM? AND IN THOSE AREAS OF YOUR LIFE WHERE YOU'VE DONE THAT, HAVE YOU EXPERIENCED ANY SHAME OR GUILT, EITHER EXTERNAL OR INTERNAL? IF SO, HOW DID YOU MANAGE THAT?

Definitely becoming my family's breadwinner. It's not something I ever wanted or thought I could do.

Growing up, my biggest dream was to find the right person to settle down with and have a family, which I did. This is what I've always wanted. This is my dream. How could I ever ask for more?

But that wasn't all there was for me. My husband's construction company career was really hard on his body, and after multiple surgeries, he had to stop.

My whole adult life, I had clung to security and what was easy. Now I didn't have that choice anymore. I had to step out and do what needed to be done. I was terrified.

But I just kept going because my husband physically could not go out and pound the pavement to get a job.

My journey to becoming the breadwinner was rocky. I wasn't living my life because I worked all the time.

So, I did the only thing that I could do. I fired all my clients and took a position inside an agency, where I ran Facebook ads and wrote ad copy for a year.

After about eight months with this ads agency, I had so many private clients for copywriting that I knew I had another choice to make. I chose to grow my own business, and we tripled our monthly income.

I figured out what I wanted to do and what I was good at. There were some breakdowns, but breakthroughs followed them, and I got my life back.

HOW DO YOU TAP INTO YOUR DIVINE FEMININE AND WILD SIDE EACH DAY?

I like to express myself through clothes. When I show up, and I'm looking nice and wearing something that complements me, it really helps me feel like a person, not just a service provider or a coach. I get regular massages, and I take care of my nails.

I also like to target shoot, ride go-karts, practice kickboxing, and own goats. It's this random collection of strange things that I giggle and just have a fun time with when I do them.

Anytime I can do something physical that reminds me I'm strong and capable, and that my body can get me from point A to point B without dying, that feeds me internally, too.

I try to not put too much pressure on myself to keep perfection around the house. When I was growing up, especially as a teenager, I was a real perfectionist.

My husband helped me a lot with this, because he just doesn't care what other people think. As I started seeing the way people love him even though he doesn't care what other people think, I began releasing my grip on feeling like I always had to come across as perfect.

I realized that people like the real Christa better than they like the perfect Christa.

Perfect Christa wasn't really a very good friend because she was always thinking about herself and how she was coming across, instead of really being there for the people she was with. People just like real people.

DUALITY DARE

Breadwinner

Our culture's masculine and feminine narrative is so closely tied to who brings home the bacon that it can pigeonhole women. The current traditional roles of women in a family unit imply we best serve as the caregiver and nurturer. We're not capable or intrinsically worthy of being the breadwinner.

I was a single mom for a long time, but it wasn't by choice; it was by force. I had no other option except to be the breadwinner.

Even though Christa tells us she originally did not want to be the breadwinner, she proved to herself that becoming the breadwinner is what she actually wanted. But it took being pushed into another narrative--one that took her outside cultural norms--for her to realize it.

Christa also discovered that not only could she be a wonderful mom and wife, like she always wanted, she also became a multi-passionate entrepreneur and her family's breadwinner. There wasn't an OR. Instead, she created an "AND" and reshaped her identity into a massive mission.

This non-traditional role of becoming the provider AND nurturer allowed her to remember her true essence. Her feminine and masculine both serve her highest good.

In what ways are you currently living into a traditional narrative, either with your partnership or in your life, that might not serve your highest good? Are there barriers and walls that would allow you a different opportunity or possibility if broken?

For this Duality Dare, write down one way you were conditioned to live in a traditional role. How does this feel to YOU?

Now flip it. For example, if you traditionally take a back seat role in meetings, why not break that tradition during the next office meeting and ask a supervisor if you can lead the meeting this month? Volunteer to present your ideas first. Speak up first with feedback.

I dare you to break one traditional behavior, role or activity that doesn't feel aligned with your Truth and see what it feels like to bravely throw yourself a curveball. Be curious about how it feels to break up the mundane tradition that isn't serving you.

CHAPTER 13

DEALER
MIA BOLDEN

Mia Bolden went from a six figure drug dealer to a six figure empowerment business coach and motivational speaker. Her mission is to help women believe in themselves, and see that they can overcome or do anything they set their minds to.

I moved from Pensacola, Florida, to North Carolina when I was 18. While I was bartending and waiting tables, a cousin of mine was selling drugs. He said to me, "Well, I can get you some real money," and he introduced me to the drug game.

I started living that fast life of just making money, partying all night, and spending money like crazy. That's how I spent most of my 20s-- bartending, waiting tables, and selling drugs.

When I was about 28, everybody around me started going to jail, including my cousin, who'd supplied me with the drugs I sold.

I had to call my mom at age 30 and ask her to come home. I was in a really bad rut. My self-confidence and self-esteem were low, and I had hit my heaviest weight of 300 pounds.

I wanted to find a fun way to work out and feel good about myself. A friend of mine, a Zumba instructor, invited me to start a burlesque class with her, which I did.

Eventually, I opened up my studio, fell in love with yoga, and we started offering all these fun fitness classes for ladies. In these classes, ladies started asking how I built my confidence up, how I started feeling good about myself, and how I lost weight.

I just shared my journey with them, which I enjoyed. A colleague of mine suggested I look into coaching. I got certified through ICF, the International Coaching Federation.

I started as a body image and confidence coach, then transitioned to empowerment business coaching.

HOW DO YOU DEFINE A MODERN WOMAN?

My definition would be somebody that can help transform another person's life for the better.

A modern woman is also one who knows her past is not her current story. That's what I tell people I coach. People will tell me, "I didn't graduate." "I had a bad upbringing." "I was the black sheep of the family."

All that's your past. It's a part of your story, but it's not your whole story. It's not who you are today. You can evolve and do different things.

I tell people, learn from your story, and try to inspire the next person. Maybe the reason you went through whatever it is you went through is to help and inspire the next person.

I know that power of belief, because I needed that. I needed somebody to believe in me when I was going through my transition--someone to say, "Mia, you can do this. You can change your life. You can keep going."

A lot of us mold ourselves based on what our family does, or what we should do. If we don't mold ourselves based on those things, we feel like a failure. That's how I felt.

I needed somebody to believe in me and say, "No, Mia, that's just a part of your story. That's not who you are," and to really believe in and motivate me.

That's why I do what I do, and why I tell people, it doesn't matter where you've been or what story you had. You can do it.

IN WHAT AREAS OF YOUR LIFE HAVE YOU STEPPED OUT OF CULTURAL NORMS, DEFIED THEM, OR GONE AGAINST THEM? AND IN THOSE AREAS OF YOUR LIFE WHERE YOU'VE DONE THAT, HAVE YOU EXPERIENCED ANY SHAME OR GUILT, EITHER EXTERNAL OR INTERNAL? IF SO, HOW DID YOU MANAGE THAT?

One thing I did was surround myself with a woman who was not only my aunt; she was my motivator, my cheerleader, my coach, and a mentor of mine. You have to get around somebody who believes in you.

You can't let guilt and that shame fester inside of you. The shame will shrink when you share it out loud.

Many people hold guilt and shame inside. We don't want to express it to anybody. We don't want to tell anybody.

But telling someone is exactly how you free yourself from guilt and shame. It's good to have a tribe, but find at least one person you trust that you can talk to--someone you know won't judge you and has your best interest at heart.

Nine times out of ten, when you share, somebody will say, "Oh, well, let me tell you about this." And then they share their story, and you realize you're not the only one going through it.

Some people think they're in it by themselves, and nobody will listen, and nobody understands, and people will judge.

You're not in it alone. There's somebody out there who will listen to you.

You have to believe in the belief others have in you before your own belief kicks in. You can grow from that. It manifests into whom you're truly supposed to be.

That's how I dealt with it, and that's how I tell everybody else to do it.

HOW DO YOU TAP INTO YOUR DIVINE FEMININE AND WILD SIDE EACH DAY?

I own a women's vertical pole fitness studio, and for a long time, that helped me tap into my feminine side. But over the years, I stopped feeling feminine during our classes.

It's still fun, but I'm more like a big kid who loves swinging on the pole than a woman experiencing her feminine side.

What got me back in touch with my feminine energy was a boudoir shoot because I felt like I was losing it.

Someone suggested one to me. I'd never done one before.

It was definitely out of my comfort zone. But afterwards, I felt that feminine energy come back. I felt so beautiful. I highly recommend a boudoir shoot to tap into your feminine side.

Vertical pole classes do that for our clients, especially for my power leaders, and the ones who always have to be type A, or in that leadership role. Or they're in a male-dominant field.

Our classes also help women who are worried about their kids, their spouse, their work and everything else, and they forget about themselves.

Everything women say they get out of these classes, it happened for me in that boudoir shoot. I loved it because I did it for me.

Same thing with these classes. Don't do it for anybody else; it's for you.

DUALITY DARE

Dealer

From a drug dealer riddled with shame to a belief builder full of confidence, Mia touches on a subject with deep roots: The cords that bind us to our past, our old identities, and the beliefs that can hold us hostage in our own minds.

Shame is tricky and icky, and it will finally be silenced when you allow it to be seen. A mentor once said to me, you will never fully evolve until you can publicly declare your deepest, darkest secrets and shame for the world to hear.

When we give our shame a voice, we set it free, and that's when our souls can truly ascend and embrace our divine purpose with clarity and confidence.

I don't want to carry shame. It's heavy and keeps us small. If I was afraid of what people would discover about me, I would always be afraid to speak my truth. If I had secrets and darkness untold, I would always be afraid to use my voice--to speak up, stand up, and be seen.

I would also always fear that someone would come out and speak against me, or tell stories about my secrets and shame.

But if I could get ahead of that, speak out my shame, and surrender myself to truly being transparent and seen, I could use my voice to step into my power and speak my truth.

When you are fully transparent, no one can disempower you. You hold the keys to your freedom.

You can unlock the dragons you have been hiding in the dungeons and be fearless in your pursuit of your vision and purpose, or you can hide from the possibility of being fully seen, and never know the full potential inside of you that's waiting to be set free.

Your Duality Dare is to look at that thing that's causing you shame...the secret holding you hostage, the cords tethering you to your past.

Identify it, and acknowledge that although it's dark, you have the power to transmute it and alchemize it into light.

Your Dare is to speak it out loud, then speak it to someone you trust, and allow them to hold a sacred safe space for you to share your secret shame.

If you do not have a safe person to hold space for you, or you're not ready for that, I encourage you to write the secret down in your journal. Then tear it out, crumple it into a ball, take it to the backyard, and burn it. I use an old coffee tin can. I place the balled up paper inside, light a match, and as the paper goes up in flames, I say out loud, "With this smoke, I choose to cut the energetic cords of shame."

CHAPTER 14

HABITS
CHANTEL RAY

Chantel is an entrepreneur, real estate queen, author, and podcaster, as well as a mom and wife. She is the president and CEO of Chantel Ray Realty, a national company present in 10 states, with a goal to be present in all fifty states within the next year.

In addition to being present in all fifty states, we also want to become a publicly traded company within six months.

I also love to write. I've written four books, and the latest is called One Meal And A Tasting. I interviewed thousands of women who have been thin their whole lives, and asked what they eat. It turns out most were eating one meal and a tasting.

I'm very motivated to make money because my goal is to give 90% of my income away. I want to make huge impacts with the amount of money I want to give to the church.

That goal is so big, and so huge, that if I was just doing it for myself, I would have already quit. But it's not just for me. I need to earn a lot of money to be able to reach the amount of people I want to reach.

One of the things people ask me is, how will you get there? There are a lot of factors, including surrounding myself with people whose values align with mine.

The people I hang out with are all significantly involved in their church. They're all succeeding in some area of life. They're very disciplined in their eating. They all work out. They live beneath their means financially. They're incredibly generous.

It's _so_ important to have people in your life who embody the same things you want for your life.

HOW DO YOU DEFINE A MODERN WOMAN?

It's based on whom you want to become. Everyone wants to accomplish the same goals: Be in great health, in great shape, be generous, have great relationships, make a difference in this world, and be financially strong. I don't know anyone who wants to be in terrible health, be really overweight, be stingy, or be in massive debt.

That's what I want, to be at the top of my game with health, relationships, my relationship to God, my ability to make a difference in this world, and my ability to be financially strong and wealthy. But I want to be extraordinarily generous, more generous than any other person I know. I don't want any other human to be able to say, "I'm more generous than Chantel."

Many people think their small decisions don't matter, but I realized every small decision I make is a big deal.

One thing people do is say, "Oh, well, one Twinkie, and one extra piece of cake. And one little thing here is not going to make a difference."

It's not that one thing. It's a multitude of one thing over time, over the years. Then they gain 30 pounds and think, wait a minute. How did this happen?

I go through all my decisions and make sure I'm making the best decision every step of the way. I also focus on who I want to become, not just what I want to do.

IN WHAT AREAS OF YOUR LIFE HAVE YOU STEPPED OUT OF CULTURAL NORMS, DEFIED THEM, OR GONE AGAINST THEM? AND IN THOSE AREAS OF YOUR LIFE WHERE YOU'VE DONE THAT, HAVE YOU EXPERIENCED ANY SHAME OR GUILT, EITHER EXTERNAL OR INTERNAL? IF SO, HOW DID YOU MANAGE THAT?

One thing is my determination to push through even when it's tough. Sometimes people make a goal at New Year's, then by Valentine's Day, 90% of those people aren't where they want to be.

One of the reasons is because you'll do it for a little, but then you don't see results. After a few weeks, things get hard, and you have no results to show for it, so you say, forget it, I'm done.

Then you have people who, even when they don't get results right away, keep doing it. That's me.

I'm frustrated now because I want growth for Chantel Ray Realty, and getting into more states is a real challenge. All the startup paperwork is a grind.

I could easily think, we're in 10 states, that's good enough. We don't have to get to all 50. But I'm not. I'll keep going until we're in all 50 states.

What helps is to create that objective outside of yourself, a goal that's bigger than you. My goal is about the number of people that I want to make an impact on.

I have two personal goals I haven't achieved: to get a private plane and to visit places I haven't been. I want to go to Israel. Other than the private plane, there's nothing else I want, materially.

Again, my goal is to give 90% of my income away. That's a huge undertaking and where I want to put all my energy. I need to earn a lot of money.

HOW DO YOU TAP INTO YOUR DIVINE FEMININE AND WILD SIDE EACH DAY?

I create habits that help me feel good about myself. I have a spa inside my house and a girl who comes to give me facials regularly. I have a girl that blow dries my hair every day.

Every four weeks, someone comes to do my hair. A girl comes to do a manicure and a pedicure. I don't have to think about it. It's already on the calendar.

Someone comes and gives me a massage at the house at least twice a week, sometimes three or four times a week.

That's what I like to spend my money on, because outside of my time with God and filling myself up spiritually, my confidence level is the most important factor in how I feel.

When I feel good about myself, that gives me confidence, and I can do so much more.

Even when I work from home, I'm not getting on a Zoom call with my hair looking undone and no makeup on because I won't feel good about myself.

I also eliminate or stay away from the things and people that chip away from my confidence. This includes taking care of myself.

If I look like 12 million bucks, but I'm a complete mess financially, in horrible relationships, and extremely overweight, I won't feel good about myself.

Every day I examine how I can get better in an area of my life. Just add one new discipline to your routine. Once it becomes a habit, it's pretty easy to do.

DUALITY DARE
Habits

Habits are a part of building the life of your dreams. Habits that seem small add up over time, and they're not just important when building a massive real estate company.

Habits can be created for every area of your life--your self-care, your femininity, your relationships, and your career or business.

How many habits do you currently have that are serving you? Count them. How many daily habits or rituals do you have that support the highest version of yourself? What do you do daily that contributes to your overall vision of becoming the best version of you? Go through your habits and write down the ones not serving your highest good.

What could you do to replace the habit of not serving yourself and creating a more positive result? For example, I used to drink wine every night, even when I didn't want it and didn't like the taste. Over time it became part of my habitual dinner routine.

Then I realized it was making me foggy. It wasn't serving my highest good. I wasn't thinking clearly, and at some point, I used it as a crutch.

When I decided to break that habit, I knew I needed to replace it with something else. Instead of drinking wine, I replaced it with sparkling water in a wine glass every night (holding that fancy wine glass was part of the habit). Then I shifted to a regular glass.

A year-and-a-half later, I still haven't had a glass of wine. Replacing the wine glass contents with fancy water was a great substitute that served my highest good and kept me clear, focused and present.

Small shifts in your habits add up and can make a huge impact on your life.

Your Duality Dare is to look at your list of habits. Identify which ones are serving you, and which ones are not. Can you replace one habit that is no longer serving you with one that is, even if you have to create a new one as I did?

Or add more of the good habits that are already serving you to replace one that isn't. Do it today. Create a new habit routine that will serve the highest version of yourself.

CHAPTER 15

SASSY
HALLIE AVOLIO

Hallie Avolio is the founder and CEO of Sassy Healthy Fit and creator of the brand Sassy as Fuck Academy, which includes a book, TV, and Sassy AF audio experience.

I grew up in this fairly traditional lifestyle. I graduated high school, graduated college in four years, and got a job in corporate America.

I was supposed to climb that corporate ladder, find the love of my life, get married, buy the house with a white picket fence--the same story we've all been told.

I did almost all those things. I've been with my amazing husband for 18 years. We have three amazing, beautiful, intelligent, wonderful children. We bought the dream home.

Yet I wasn't happy. I wasn't joyful. I wasn't living in passion, or with purpose.

When I hit my mid-30s, I felt really disgruntled and frustrated. I asked myself, what the fuck am I doing in my life? What is this even for?

A more sane person might have sought positive reinforcement and help, but I went the other way. I sewed some oats and embraced a wild child self-destruction phase.

It's what I had to do to get to the place I'm at now, at age 41, which is realizing that I have a passion and a purpose. I deeply understand who I am at my core.

Being sassy as fuck means living a life you love that's authentic to you. It also means having fun and not feeling guilty about it.

Also, you don't have to hustle. You don't have to fight and claw your way to the top. I lived that life, and it sucked, physically and mentally. Life can be about flow and ease.

HOW DO YOU DEFINE A MODERN WOMAN?

It's a woman who stands on her own two feet. She's not worrying about what others are doing, or what they think of her.

Yet, she also understands that she works better as part of a community. She knows their success doesn't take away from hers, and vice versa.

We don't need more competition; we need more love. Lead with love. Come from a heart space in everything you do because you cannot go wrong when you do that.

I choose love every day, but I know what tools I need in terms of staying in that practice. For me, I have to follow a morning ritual. And my morning ritual is what I use to fill my cup before I deal with anything else. For me, it includes meditation and journaling, and often movement.

Throughout the day, I say affirmations regularly and take walks as often as I can, literally getting out of my house, enjoying nature, and being outside in the fresh air.

I also love connecting with people that fill me up. I've weeded out a lot of people in my life who weren't good for me.

Now I gravitate towards people who infuse me with this amazing, vibrant energy. When I need a boost, I'll just pick up my phone and leave a little voice message that says, "Hey, I just wanted to say hi. I wanted to send you some love." Doing that with no expectation of return fills me with more vibrant energy.

IN WHAT AREAS OF YOUR LIFE HAVE YOU STEPPED OUT OF CULTURAL NORMS, DEFIED THEM, OR GONE AGAINST THEM? AND IN THOSE AREAS OF YOUR LIFE WHERE YOU'VE DONE THAT, HAVE YOU EXPERIENCED ANY SHAME OR GUILT, EITHER EXTERNAL OR INTERNAL? IF SO, HOW DID YOU MANAGE THAT?

Not stepping outside cultural norms brought me to this place of massive resentment and frustration because I wasn't actually aligned with who I am.

One of the ways I've kind of broken off from that is starting my own business, developing this brand, and going with the mindset of "I am sassy as fuck." It's pretty out there.

I'm very active on LinkedIn, and LinkedIn is a more conservative, professional platform, from a business perspective. Yet my headline on LinkedIn says, "I am a sassy as f*ck lifestyle designer."

You don't see that a lot on LinkedIn. I don't have any shame or guilt around it, and it does attract people to me. It also turns off some people, and that's okay. Those people will find someone else who resonates with them.

I've also made a decision that I will not feel shame and guilt, but it's been a long time coming. I ended up living this very complacent life that wasn't filling me up. That's one of the repercussions of living for outside expectations. Now I've chosen to stand in my power and be who I am.

When you're doing any of this work, you have to have massive compassion for yourself. When you can have that massive self-awareness and compassion, self-love comes, and the pleasure starts to increase.

HOW DO YOU TAP INTO YOUR DIVINE FEMININE AND WILD SIDE EACH DAY?

My wild woman absolutely comes out through dance and music I love. When I can let go and release and get out of here, I get out of my head and into my heart space.

It also happens when I can get deeper into my body--into that root chakra and sacral chakra. In that space, I feel alive and invigorated and primal and vibrant.

Same when I dance and listen to music. I've got several playlists I tap into, depending on my mood. I've got my hot sexy one. I've got a sassy as fuck one.

Sometimes I like a more mellow vibe, so I'll go that way too. But feeling the music and moving my body, especially if I can be barefoot, does it for me.

Last year I took a striptease class through a pole dancing studio, and let me tell you, that was so fun. Talk about tapping into your primal side!

We were practicing with other people in the class, mostly women, and you have to let your guard down and allow yourself to be in your body, so you can move in these sensual ways that feel wild and free.

It was a six-week series, and at the end, I performed for my husband in the sanctity of our own home, and it was fabulous. I don't know how good I am at it. I'm not ready to get a job in that world. But it was amazing and so fun.

DUALITY DARE

Sassy

Sassy As Fuck, wild and free is how Hallie shows up as a modern woman. What does sassy mean to you?

I think it can mean different things at different times in our life. As a girl, I connected the word sassy with bratty or precocious. As a teenager, I associated the word with outspoken. As a young woman, I associated it with being bold.

As a woman in my forties, I feel that sassy is a collection of wisdom with no boundaries. Our inner knowing just flows and speaks loudly, unfiltered and unapologetic, and doesn't seek approval.

Sass can be audacious or gentle, but inherently it elicits a powerful response and gets me fired up, ready to use my voice and speak up for my values, opinions, and desires.

If someone described you as sassy as fuck today, what would you be creating, speaking, or wearing? How would you be acting?

Your Duality Dare is to get out your journal and create a sass list. What ways of being would make you feel sassy? How would you dress? What would you say? What fantasy would you act out with your partner?

Once you've got your list, close your eyes and use your finger to point to one of the sassy descriptions. Guess what? You get to put that into action and become sassy as fuck today!

CHAPTER 16

UNSHAKABLE
JEN WILLIAMSON

Jen Williamson is a certified life coach and entrepreneur. She's spent two decades perfecting how to bridge the gap between the life you have and the life you want.

We all have that moment or season where our whole lives change. For me, that moment came when I joined the Navy at 18 years old.

Back then, I had every single bad habit you can imagine. I took a laxative because I was overweight. I smoked cigarettes. I drank alcohol. I ate at McDonald's.

I'm not kidding--if there was a bad habit, I had it.

But when I joined the Navy, suddenly, it was this total clean slate. From there, I rebuilt my life.

I grew to understand the power of structure, habits, morning routines, and discipline.

I also went from being the heavy, "not smart" girl to the pretty, smart girl quickly. That's what changed on the outside. On the inside, I'd changed my beliefs about myself.

When people tell me, "I'm not getting this, and I'm not getting that," or "You're not giving me this or you're not giving me that," I say, "Be the gap. Be what's missing. If you want love, be love. If you want patience, be patient. If you want affection, you give affection." Be the gap.

HOW DO YOU DEFINE A MODERN WOMAN?

It's somebody who is authentically and unapologetically themselves.

I used to hold myself back because I was so afraid of being judged or criticized and not looking good. Now I get to unapologetically be me, which permits other people to be unapologetically themselves.

Being unapologetically me also shows people that I'm enough and that I can be authentically myself and also be congruent.

By congruent, I mean the way you show up professionally is also how you show up behind closed doors. If it's not congruent, it does seep out.

I've never been the person threatened by other people's success. I was always motivated by it. Oh, that's the next cut.

As the saying goes, if you want to be a tall tree in the forest, you can either spend your time chopping down all the other trees or spend your time growing.

The way I grow my tree is by being around other successful ones. Nothing makes me happier than seeing other people's success.

I also think a modern woman is someone who goes for what she authentically wants, whatever that looks like for her.

She doesn't hit the snooze button because if you're hitting that snooze on your alarm, you're hitting snooze on your life, right?

If you're saying I'll do it tomorrow, you're also pushing your goals and dreams to tomorrow. Go after what you want starting today.

IN WHAT AREAS OF YOUR LIFE HAVE YOU STEPPED OUT OF CULTURAL NORMS, DEFIED THEM, OR GONE AGAINST THEM? AND IN THOSE AREAS OF YOUR LIFE WHERE YOU'VE DONE THAT, HAVE YOU EXPERIENCED ANY SHAME OR GUILT, EITHER EXTERNAL OR INTERNAL? IF SO, HOW DID YOU MANAGE THAT?

I'm hyper aware of guilt and shame being very low-vibration, so if I feel a tinge of that, I can quickly get out of it.

What I teach people is how to have a super strong emotional immune system. We've all heard the saying, fill your bucket. I say <u>we</u> are the bucket, and when we're dumping all this great stuff into us from our morning routine, our mentality, our vision boards, and so on, then our bucket is full of great things. We're filled with gratitude, abundance, possibility, and love. There's no room for guilt and shame.

I call that being unshakable. It's where you're so full. There's just no room for things like guilt and shame. They may come in for a second, but because you're so full of good things--because your emotional immune system is so strong--they're diluted.

We are not the thoughts. We are the thinker of our thoughts. When you see yourself that way, one negative thought is not going to turn into five thousand. Instead, you can flip it into a positive possibility.

The moment we open our eyes in the morning, we start filling the bucket. So I wake up and go immediately into gratitude. I have a bench at the end of my bed, and on my way to use the bathroom, I drop to my knees and pray. Then I go into what I call PMJ - pray, meditate, and journal.

We're not perfect. But we get to be proactive instead of reactive. We get to be the best versions of ourselves.

94

HOW DO YOU TAP INTO YOUR DIVINE FEMININE AND WILD SIDE EACH DAY?

I'm a girly girl by nature. I'm a powerful woman in business and life, but I'm very feminine. I love to have pretty clothing. I just love pretty! It doesn't even have to be me. I even love beautiful women. My house is pretty, and my clothes are pretty.

If I ever want to make myself feel better in the moment, I look at pretty houses or pretty hair.

It's funny because in the Navy, we wear the exact same uniform. We were discouraged from wearing much makeup. Our hair had to be in a bun or cut really short.

So, I wore pretty panties. Every time I went to the bathroom, they reminded me I was a pretty girl.

I bring a lot of that femininity to my husband. My husband's a very masculine guy, a G.I. Joe, a renaissance man. I like to bring pretty to him.

I'm also very silly. He'll be all serious, working on a spreadsheet, and I'll walk up and lift up my sweater with my boobs hanging out.

The other thing that I do every single morning is look at a picture of myself when I was about five years old and ask, am I living the life she would want me to?

It's part of my morning routine, keeps me grounded in whom God made me to be, before the world told me who to be, before the world told me what to wear, what to like or what to buy.

DUALITY DARE

Unshakable

When we learn to fill our own buckets, we become unshakable. How can you learn to fill your own buckets and create your uncompromised emotional immune system, as Jen shares?

Jen's PMJ (pray meditate journal) method is how she fills her bucket and creates a strong emotional immune system. It's such a relatable take on the "morning routine" we all hear about.

We all have strategies we're drawn to and instinctively want to create in the mornings, but so many things get in our way.

For this Duality Dare, start creating your morning routine based on your instincts. What are three things you're drawn to creating every morning before you get out of bed that will strengthen your emotional immune system and allow you to become unshakable?

Jen's method may work perfectly for you, or it may not. I personally need to get physically active in the morning to feel my best. That's part of my morning recipe and how I fill my bucket.

Write down five ways you think creating a morning routine would impart a stronger emotional immune system for you. What are five things you can do that would fill your day and your bucket?

Tomorrow, try out three of them and see how it feels. If something doesn't feel right, create a different recipe until you find one that truly allows you to feel stable, strong, and unshakeable.

CHAPTER 17

LIBERATION
KEELIN CLARK

Keelin Clark is an empowerment coach, transformational leadership coach, and the founder of Liberty Empowerment. Keelin is committed to empowering humans for a peaceful world through liberation, creativity, and joy.

I worked in corporate for twenty years. After my first year in college, I decided to major in partying.

Alcoholics raised me. They were loving, fun, generous people who were also alcoholics, and they raised a really, really successful alcoholic.

After college, I went into the world and just started working. I had a great career full of great learning experiences.

The problem was, over those twenty years, I was starving my artist because I was always too afraid to become a starving artist.

Instead, I did the opposite. Yes, I had a career for twenty years, but I was always searching, and doing so in places that probably weren't healthy, like partying. I really limited myself.

In 2018, I decided to get sober--not just concerning alcohol but also on so many different levels. I liberated myself from starving my artist, and all the consequences of doing that.

I started doing the internal work, the really hard work.

Since then I have taken a stand for liberation in creativity and joy, because there's so much of both to be had out there.

HOW DO YOU DEFINE A MODERN WOMAN?

What it means to me is to be self-expressive, and powerfully honor who I am. I do that by dyeing my hair in different colors. I do that by speaking my mind online. I do that by empowering other people to get their videos and their businesses online.

On my journey to remember who I am, I did much internal work. Remembering who you are is being able to be with yourself.

Every day I get intimate with myself on so many levels, to the point of just being able to meditate for 15-20 minutes. The remembering comes from the inside.

There are things we can do on the outside, like having conversations. But that reflective alone time is when we can really start permitting ourselves to remember.

It's also important to honor what makes you uncomfortable, yet you know it is your truth. Whatever it is. I could be your intuitive powers. It could be wanting to dress like a man. It could be anything, but it's really the honoring of yourself.

I remember a quote a yoga teacher told me years ago. She said, "that higher higher power, that inner knowing, is when you know that you know that you know."

I think we, as women, all have that. We just turn it off. When we turn off our light and our sensuality, we turn off our creativity, right? We turn all of it off.

We're so caught up with the wanting of that connection that we don't realize it's already there.

IN WHAT AREAS OF YOUR LIFE HAVE YOU STEPPED OUT OF CULTURAL NORMS, DEFIED THEM, OR GONE AGAINST THEM? AND IN THOSE AREAS OF YOUR LIFE WHERE YOU'VE DONE THAT, HAVE YOU EXPERIENCED ANY SHAME OR GUILT, EITHER EXTERNAL OR INTERNAL? IF SO, HOW DID YOU MANAGE THAT?

Liberation. Liberation is freeing ourselves from giving an eff what other people think and being true to ourselves. I started by dyeing my hair, beginning with one little extension that was bright blue. It felt so risky. But I showed up to my corporate office with bright blue hair, and they all loved it. So, it was me pushing the envelope over and over again.

I was raised by two feminists, my godmother and my mom. They're from the late 60s and 70s, and my mom had tickets to Woodstock. They really ingrained in me that you don't change your last name.

Then I got engaged, and I decided that's not my story. I love this guy. So I changed my name. It's not the patriarchal idea of it. It's to honor him and his family, and live in a house where everyone has the same last name. I never lived there before.

It's an old school way for me to think, but not changing my name was taking on someone else's story. There's so much data and so much noise and so many "right" ways to do things.

As modern women, we get to be free. We get to do what honors us.

Getting through the shame and guilt is going back to just really being in tune with yourself, right? At first, it's weird, it's hard, and you lose people.

But the ones that get you and understand you, they're not going anywhere.

HOW DO YOU TAP INTO YOUR DIVINE FEMININE AND WILD SIDE EACH DAY?

I love writing. I love painting. I love being an artist. For years I used alcohol to fulfill that. When I decided to use my powers for good, I realized I didn't know how to have fun without the booze. I changed that by asking, "Okay, what am I denying myself by drinking?"

The divine feminine is something I have really explored in just the last couple of years, and it was hard. I grew up as an only child and got picked on by many girls who are still my friends.

In high school, I was closer to and liked being friends with guys. I always thought girls were kind of mean. When I went to college, I had girlfriends for the first time. I embraced it more when I was in my 20s and then even more in my 30s. It's an exploration of tapping into the divine feminine.

I also join healing circles. I have several women in my life who are shamans and energy healers, and through that, I've been able to honor my own wisdom and my own gifts. I also love going on camera.

Tapping into my divine feminine is about asking, what can I lean into today? What do I want to tap into? And putting myself in that creative space.

DUALITY DARE

Liberation

Casting the spell of liberty through a camera is how Keelin shows up as a modern woman. She encourages women to be seen instead of intimidated. She encourages women to go back through our ancestral history and start to poke at the patriarchy from a position of power and owning our own duality.

As women, we can be creative, free and wild without fear of being threatened or persecuted.

There was a moment in my interview with Keelin that really gave me goosebumps. She was told that women who feel threatened shave their heads. At that moment, she realized her head was shaved into a mohawk.

As women, we have been persecuted for desiring liberty, freedom, autonomy, and sovereignty, and actually burned at the stake for thousands of years for expressing ourselves. It's in our bones to protect ourselves. How then can we start to cut those cords of ancestral trauma, and create freedom and liberation?

Now it's time to ask yourself this very intimate question: What are you truly protecting yourself from? Your head might not be shaved, but are you hiding in big clothing? Are you hiding behind excess weight? Are you trying to waste away to be invisible by over-exercising or dieting? Anything to avoid not being seen for who and what you really are.

First, write down this affirmation and say it out loud: I am safe and secure just as I am.

Next, write down two ways you might be protecting yourself. Then create an opportunity to be exposed without the protection you've created, so your logical mind can anchor to evidence.

For example, if you hide at parties or events and become a wallflower, next time there is an event, instead, stand in the center of the room. Then reflect on what happened? Are you still safe after being exposed? Anchor to that safety and move forward.

Create two unique ways you can break through the self-protection barrier, then take action on one immediately.

CHAPTER 18

PLEASURE
WENDY PETTIES

Wendy Petties is an author, founder of the brand Sexy Money, a personal trainer for your money, and the host of a financial wellness retreat.

I'm a native New Yorker through and through, who now has lived and moved to Las Vegas.

I know, who does that? But it makes sense given all the things that make up who I am. My whole brand is about sexy money.

I do everything with my instinct, but mainly I moved to Las Vegas because I wanted to be warm. Plus, I have friends and family here. If I'm going to be in a pandemic, I want a much bigger house than my house in New York, and so that's why I'm here.

What jazzes me and juices me up is true connection. It's about figuring out what you want, knowing you can have it and that you're worth it, and getting it.

In all of your choices, you decide what it is you're going to have. Everything you have is because you're being a certain way and doing certain things--both the good and the bad.

You can't just claim all the accolades. All the crap, that's you, too, but I don't mean that from a place of shame. I don't do shame. The good and the bad both, I honor it, with grace.

HOW DO YOU DEFINE A MODERN WOMAN?

It means to be valued and worthy and full. It means to be present in this moment because modern for me is being attentive and focused on what's happening now, and not reflecting so much about the past or about where you're going. Being present in the moment has been my go-to, especially in times of trauma.

I love being a woman. And I'm so different from other women and so connected in other ways to women.

As women, we are designed for pleasure. Many people don't know that.

I say that we need to learn some things we were never taught. We need to unlearn some things we were taught that were just wrong, and we need to question what we really believe.

We need to talk about these things. We need to infuse these things into our lives.

Whatever view you come from, just do it. Whatever pleasure means to you, whatever joy means to you, make it part of your life. That's how I've changed my whole life.

IN WHAT AREAS OF YOUR LIFE HAVE YOU STEPPED OUT OF CULTURAL NORMS, DEFIED THEM, OR GONE AGAINST THEM? AND IN THOSE AREAS OF YOUR LIFE WHERE YOU'VE DONE THAT, HAVE YOU EXPERIENCED ANY SHAME OR GUILT, EITHER EXTERNAL OR INTERNAL? IF SO, HOW DID YOU MANAGE THAT?

In the areas of sex and money both. From a sex standpoint, I've openly dated multiple men at the same time. Some people have a problem

104

with that. It's a cultural taboo, and people would rather we be divorced.

People make up stories about how you're supposed to behave based on how they would do it or how they think they should do it.

I stepped out of the cultural restraints around money by telling the truth. I filed for bankruptcy. I was ill for a number of years and racked up $310,000 in medical bills. I made a lot of money working on Wall Street, which is how I paid for my house, but I couldn't help some of the other things. I had a lot of shame when I filed for bankruptcy.

After I left Wall Street, I was the in-house executive coach for JetBlue Airways. I loved it, but it paid me half of my salary. So, I started talking about it and asking questions, not hiding behind it like so many people do. Now I'm worth $1.2 million, and I say it proudly.

I've always said about my relationships, money, and damn near anything else, you can't out me. If there are naked pictures, and you find them, I'm going to show you the rest of them. I refuse to be shamed by other people. I've worked through that.

To express yourself in a way that you are fully yourself is so juicy and yummy. I wish that for everybody. You don't have to date multiple people to do that. Make choices for yourself.

HOW DO YOU TAP INTO YOUR DIVINE FEMININE AND WILD SIDE EACH DAY?

I focus on what I was designed for: Pleasure, and finding ways to bring myself back to that in all ways.

For example, I went to IKEA to look at a desk I wanted to go up and down. I bought it, but it didn't bring me joy. Then it was delayed because I believe we put energy out into the universe.

Then I went to Costco with my friend, and we're laughing and joking and sharing music in our headphones. We're turned on and turned up.

We turn a corner, and there sits a desk for half the price of the IKEA desk. I bought two because I want to be able to sit with the light on my face and work at my desk; and I want to be able to stand up and dance at that desk over there.

Pleasure starts with the five senses. It can start daily with your shower. Most of us take a shower every day, brush our teeth, wash under our arms, and wash between our legs. Your shower can be a metaphor for your entire day.

Feel whether the water is the way you like it. Smell the soap. Notice whether the puff or the washcloth you use feels good to you. Turn on some music, or not. Because sometimes the It doesn't have to cost anything. It's about tuning in.

DUALITY DARE

Pleasure

Threading pleasure through your daily life can create fun, femininity and flow. I used to get caught in my masculine so frequently that burnout was my constant state of being.

As women, we are not designed to tap into our masucline energy for long periods without breaking the force. It will zap your sex drive, your adrenals, and imbalance your hormones. Living in that state was the recipe for my life as a depressed, anxiety-ridden, bulimic, anorexic, over-exercised, exhausted business owner. This energy was the only place I believed I would be affirmed. Today I've learned a different way.

Wendy talks about how to sprinkle pleasure throughout your daily life, to bring out that feminine energy. Instead of just taking a shower for the purchase of taking a shower, take a shower for the senses. Caress your body and feel the warmth of the hot water down your neck. Allow the steam to fill you. Inhale and exhale and be present with what's bringing you pleasure.

Understanding what you desire is key to understanding your own internal guide towards your Divine Purpose. Pleasure is powerful, and performing for your own pleasure will keep you out of masculine energy and bring you into feminine energy, which is where we, as women, have the endurance to go the distance so we can create massive impact.

How can you honor your pleasure today? What small things make you smile, feel sensual, sexual, beautiful?

Your Duality Dare is to make a list in the journal section of this book of ten things that bring you pleasure. Then choose three and make them part of your day.

Before our interview together for this book, Wendy and I both went and grabbed pretty pens that were gold and heavy. Using these pens to take notes was sensual. I also surround myself with crystals, flowers, and incense while I work.

I create a little shrine wherever I am working. It includes simple things, but creates a beautiful experience. What can you add to mundane tasks to make them a beautiful, sensual experience?

CHAPTER 19

SURVIVOR
KIMBERLY MINER

Kimberly Miner is the founder and CEO of Kimberly Miner Network. She is a transformational speaker and empowerment consultant that has helped thousands of women find their self-confidence and self-esteem through the difficult journey of domestic violence.

I'm a survivor of domestic violence. After years of adversity, I've taken that spot, and I want to take that experience, take the voice I found after years of having no voice, and be a voice for so many others. I want to show them there's another side.

I also want to take my twenty-five years of corporate experience, and bring those two worlds together.

I've created curriculums and summits and a TV show to be a voice regularly.

There, I can show women how you get to that other side, empower yourself, and create opportunities for yourself.

Over and over again, I've thought that I was doing something for others. I am, but I've also realized that I'm actually the one getting the gift day after day every time I do something.

HOW DO YOU DEFINE A MODERN WOMAN?

As a modern woman, you're present. You take your power, show up, and don't allow others to be your voice.

I came from a male dominated industry, so I felt like my voice was never heard. I wanted to progress, but as a single mother, I was told, "Just keep doing your job."

I'm a single mother who was a huge multitasker. I was capable of doing many different things. To be told I was incapable of doing anything more was frustrating.

It's important we women use our voice to say, "I can do anything I choose to do." Whatever you think you can do, believe in it. Develop an action plan and figure out what you need to do to make that happen.

Stop being shy about it. If a man wants something, they're not shy about doing what it takes or voicing what they want. Why do we, as women, feel incapable of voicing what we want?

The modern day woman needs to voice what she wants and not feel bashful or embarrassed that she has things she wants to achieve.

Think of what you had to go through each day to get through the day. You have so much more resilience than you think you do. You survived. Pat yourself on the back for that.

IN WHAT AREAS OF YOUR LIFE HAVE YOU STEPPED OUT OF CULTURAL NORMS, DEFIED THEM, OR GONE AGAINST THEM? AND IN THOSE AREAS OF YOUR LIFE WHERE YOU'VE DONE THAT, HAVE YOU EXPERIENCED ANY SHAME OR GUILT, EITHER EXTERNAL OR INTERNAL? IF SO, HOW DID YOU MANAGE THAT?

I've spent my whole life against the grain. That's where I feel most comfortable. When somebody tells me, "You know what, Kim, I don't

109

think that you can probably accomplish that," I love nothing more than to say, "Watch me."

I don't fit well in that perfect little box. When I see TV or movies where they show everybody in that successful job, in that perfect office overlooking the bay or the city, and it's beautiful, I think, "Oh, that's so nice!"

Then a commercial comes, and I realize I would only last about 2.3 seconds. I just can't exist in the cookie cutter world.

I do well in the entrepreneurial world, where I create my own rules in my own boundaries to be creative. I get to exist in a world where I see a problem or something that needs to be done, and I go after it. That's where I do my best work.

I spent twenty-five years in corporate sales, even though I didn't go to an office. I worked out of my home and travelled. When I set up my own company, I had a conversation with my father. He said, "I don't understand what you've done. How is it you do all the things you do?"

In his mind, you have to follow a certain pattern to do certain things. But because I don't follow a certain pattern, I can't be doing what I'm doing, so I have to quantify what I'm doing.

HOW DO YOU TAP INTO YOUR DIVINE FEMININE AND WILD SIDE EACH DAY?

I tend for a lot of my masculinity to come out. I'm used to being in charge, raising two kids independently, and doing what needs to be done. I also have a strong personality.

When I'm with my friends, I make sure I have that laughter come out.

One thing people say about me is that I can go into any room and only know one person, but I leave the room best friends with everybody. I take that as the feminine part of me coming out. I want to socialize. I want to laugh and joke with everybody, because I love people. I care about people.

I carry my heart on my sleeve. That's the feminine part coming out. So I'm very sensitive. I love and care about people. It's why I'm good at what I do.

The biggest thing you can do is put your hand out and lift somebody else up with you. A great book I read says, "the more you give, the more you'll get back," so I try so much to give.

Being a giver has probably been my biggest attribute about myself. It's hurt me a lot in the past. I've been walked all over.

Even so, I would rather be authentic to who I am than have to change who I am.

DUALITY DARE

Survivor

Far too many women have said to me that they're surviving, without embodying the fact that they're thriving. Like Kimberly, far too many women have felt suffocated and silenced. For some, it happened through domestic abuse.

What most of us don't understand is that we're thriving. Because of our trauma and pain, we don't connect to thriving as much as we do to surviving. We wake up day after day just trying to make it through the pain, the trauma, the abuse, the deprecation. So when we're in a space in our lives where we're thriving, we sometimes don't recognize it.

I want to eradicate the word survivor from our dictionary, and replace it with the word WOMAN. All women have survived some type of persecution--effects of the patriarchy, objectification, etc.--at some level and at some point in their lives. Yet, so many of us are thriving and not recognizing how far we've come.

On the other side of the trauma, there is still so much to heal, work through, and reframe. We get to shift.

For the record, can we all please stop trying to quantify or qualify our own abuse. No abuse scale makes us worthy of identifying our pain and trauma this way. Abuse is abuse, period. You don't need permission to have pain, and you don't get to feel guilty for not having trauma as deep or painful as another woman's.

Kimberly talks about rebuilding your resilience after abuse by identifying five positive attributes about yourself every day for thirty days. I am going to ask you to start with one. Write down one thing right now that is a positive way you show up. For example, "I am generous."

If you can't think of one thing, call your mom, sister or best friend and ask them what your most positive attribute is.

Then, for your Duality Dare, I want you to develop a superhero character name that embodies that positive attribute. Using the example of generosity again, the first thing that comes to my mind is Robin Hood. Use whatever comes up for you and your positive attribute. You get to create your own.

For me, I love to embody the attribute of empowerment, and my superhero character is She-Ra, Princess of Power. She represents me at the highest version of myself. When I am self-doubt, self-depreciation, anxiety, fear, or self-sabotage, I call She-ra in and ask myself if I embody who She-ra is.

This is a great anchor for us to call forward the highest version of ourselves in a simple, fun and memorable way. If you have kids, they love this exercise!

CHAPTER 20

BRIDGE
LAURA HOLLOWAY

Laura Holloway has been an entrepreneur for over 10 years. She is an expert in health and wellness, mindfulness, and business. Laura is also the host of the Activate podcast and co-founder of One for Many.

I've called myself a certified entrepreneur since I was little. Literally certified unemployable. I think I went to one interview. I put on some pearls and did the whole interview thing. I almost threw up.

I played volleyball at Penn State and UCLA. I remember looking at all my girlfriends who were freelancing and doing different things and decided I wanted to live the lifestyle of a professional athlete without being one.

I've had four reconstructive right knee surgeries and two right shoulder surgeries. When I was out in LA, I kept asking myself, how do I keep this lifestyle where I'm healthy and active, but also free, making a lot of money, and traveling?

I approached different people and asked, what do you do, and how can I have your life? I didn't want to be in a box.

Today I'm not in a box. I am a creator, and I continue to create, which will probably evolve over the years.

HOW DO YOU DEFINE A MODERN WOMAN?

I think we're all modern women, and we're as in-demand as we choose to be, but I would say it means being a woman in today's world that's willing to show up and shine her light and share her gifts freely, and on a large scale. Share big and don't be afraid to be seen.

There are seasons in our life where we can be mothers and retreat. There are seasons of our life where we get to relax and take a break. Then there are "go-go-go" seasons where you get to build and be "on." I get to co-create.

I've been in different seasons of my life. There was one where I built a massive business in Los Angeles. I've transitioned to Chicago, and I came back because my brother was getting married. I was doing everything for everyone, and I wanted a moment to be with my family and meet a partner.

I think it's most important to be in tune with ourselves so we know what season it is. I'm in an in-demand season right now, and I feel it. It's not always that way, and it won't always be that way.

But I know it is now until I have my kids, because that's what I want. I can sense that season coming forward, when I'll be in demand for my (future) family.

IN WHAT AREAS OF YOUR LIFE HAVE YOU STEPPED OUT OF CULTURAL NORMS, DEFIED THEM, OR GONE AGAINST THEM? AND IN THOSE AREAS OF YOUR LIFE WHERE YOU'VE DONE THAT, HAVE YOU EXPERIENCED ANY SHAME OR GUILT, EITHER EXTERNAL OR INTERNAL? IF SO, HOW DID YOU MANAGE THAT?

When I was first building my business in Los Angeles, I got a lot of outside opinions. Buying into them felt limiting, dark, and suffocating. I decided it was too painful to listen to what these people say is best for me, especially when it's out of alignment with my truth.

114

I felt more sickness inside and more out of alignment by listening to those outside opinions than when I took the risks it would take to be big, listen to the call, and follow my heart.

Jim Rohn always says, when the pain of staying the same outgrows the pain of change, then you'll change. I've reached that point multiple times in my life. I wore that athlete jersey for a long time and was scared to step into a new jersey. We get scared to put on these jerseys because we're attached to the physical jersey rather than who we are inside of it.

Our soul is an ever evolving being that can bring its expression in every chapter of our lives. If you go from wellness to podcasting to politics, you're bringing you with you. You're not meant to stay the same.

The biggest thing I've had to let go of is what people think. Anybody that's judging me is judging themselves. I tell them, "listen, if I don't leave, I can't take you anywhere else." How do I be the bridge if I don't cross the bridge? I cross the bridge so I can help you cross the bridge if you choose to. I do that by example. It's hard, not easy, to be the first.

HOW DO YOU TAP INTO YOUR DIVINE FEMININE AND WILD SIDE EACH DAY?

I don't tap into it every day. When I go too long without tapping into my divine feminine, I can start to feel it in my chest area. That's when double up the divine feminine.

I do that with a massage, a cryotherapy appointment, or an infrared sauna. I take care of my health on a whole other level. I do steam, sauna, dry brush, work out, and drink a ton of water. I get enough sleep, move my body, dance, and I love to cook. I grab a girl and go to a dance class.

I'm a huge music person, so I make playlists. I love discovering new music. It taps me into my body and my hips. I light candles, turn on the fireplace, cook, and create a romantic evening for myself. Lighting and smells and sound are all part of it.

I might just chew my food differently or have a piece of chocolate with a glass of wine and really taste it.

I was an athlete, sixty percent masculine and forty percent feminine, so I have to practice these things. I surround myself with women that have that feminine energy because I want to be in its presence.

I run many women's empowerment groups, and go to female events to be around the energy. I host women's circles, and even if it's four or five people, there's something that happens when we're around each other.

I've had to retrain myself to love my feminine. Receiving a muscle I've had to practice consciously.

DUALITY DARE

Bridge

How can I be the bridge if I don't cross the bridge? How can we carve out a new path for others if we don't shift, leave the old, and start forging the new?

I think there are a lot of different contexts where we can use this analogy in. We can't be leaders if we're unwilling to leave an identity and start anew. We can't create new narratives, new frameworks, or allow ourselves to reinvent, rediscover, and redefine ideas, beliefs and patterns unless we're willing to adopt, shift, and pivot.

Leading the way for other women is a job for each of us. We can lead by example--the example of allowing our seasons and allowing ourselves to reinvent who we thought we were so that we can become who we are meant to become.

What if we're still stuck in our past, and we haven't crossed through the trauma bridge or ascended over the fear bridge? Motherhood bridge (as in Laura's case)? Or the athlete bridge?

I love this analogy of being a bridge. For your Duality Dare, I want you to create a new bridge between who you think you are and who you really are.

In the journal section of this book write down the beliefs you have about who you are. For example, at one point, I would have written my identities in this order:

"I am a bikini model, fitness trainer, and business owner."

Now go ask your son or daughter, or mother or sister, this question:

How would you describe me?

I bet the theme you'll hear from them is about who you BE, not what you DO. Maybe something like "funny, kind, supportive," etc.

Now write down everything they said on the other side of the paper. How can you bridge the gap for yourself? Today, how can you become a bridge for more laughter, kindness and support, versus something like a "better bikini model."

They will not remember what you DO, but they will remember who you BE. How can you stay in your ways of BEing? How can you create more kindness, laughter and support? Write down three ways right now, and align your to-do-list with a new version called your to-be list.

CHAPTER 21

ALCHEMY
MIA SAENZ

Mia Saenz is a love activist and creator of women making miracles. As a clairvoyant and healer, Mia helps tune into love's promise for women so they can turn on their life and become their own life's work.

As my spiritual level has grown, so have my mental and physical levels. What I've come to understand is, there's so much greatness. It comes from within and from healing the inner parts. It's there to make sure you connect with that wild, sassy, sensual, empowered, elegant, whatever you want to be woman.

My life was very rough. It was beautiful, and it was rough. But I needed it to grow and become who I am. Even in my astrological charts, it says that I'm a healer and I'm to teach love, which is crazy.

I had to have the darkness to understand the light, and I don't see my history as something negative. I see it as the blessing that has given me gifts to do anything that I want and desire.

Miracles happen every day when we not only understand and accept what we want, but allow ourselves to go for it, and to receive it when it shows up. We don't receive until we learn to receive.

We, as women, are magnificent. We can heal the wounds in our womb and be massive entrepreneurs, making so much money and nurturing and loving and supporting many people.

In our throats, we can release all the lies that have been told about us. We can release everything that has been attached to us because it's really not us.

HOW DO YOU DEFINE A MODERN WOMAN?

It's when I feel I've accomplished what I set out to do, and also that I'm still accomplishing. I treat my life as a petri dish for the betterment of humanity. I've been supporting people in equal rights since I was a little girl on the playground.

Being a modern woman is being so empowered, which you do by healing the inner dialogue, and the inner journey.

You also have to connect your Trinity--your body, mind and spirit. They have to be activated together to feel the empowerment.

You have to recognize your gifts, you have to recognize your beauty, your elegance, your feistiness, your queenhood, your gentleness. All the sparks around you are there because most of them are from wounds. But as we clear those away, what's left is the diamond. You're no longer in the rough. You're sparkling.

When I killed cancer in my body, I did a lot of research on healing myself, and in a book, I read that I needed to have a mantra, "I'm in spontaneous remission." It took me more than three days over three mala beads, to get it so that I wasn't saying, "I'm in spontaneous submission."

Once I got to "I'm in spontaneous remission," guess what? I would then tap delete in my head every time I wanted to. I would say it and even if I didn't have my mala beads, it would start to continue with the synapses. In four and a half months, these massive, stage three to four tumors were gone. You can create a beautiful mantra to support you in receiving whatever it is you want to receive.

IN WHAT AREAS OF YOUR LIFE HAVE YOU STEPPED OUT OF CULTURAL NORMS, DEFIED THEM, OR GONE AGAINST THEM? AND IN THOSE AREAS OF YOUR LIFE WHERE YOU'VE DONE THAT, HAVE YOU EXPERIENCED ANY SHAME OR GUILT, EITHER EXTERNAL OR INTERNAL? IF SO, HOW DID YOU MANAGE THAT?

I had been raped, and my first husband was not protecting me from men. He was not telling them to stop. I was afraid, so I decided to eat until no man looked at me again. It almost killed me.

I had to redefine my body, myself, and my life. I realized that I do carry weight--I'm naturally a buxom woman. I did gain some weight because of the cancer and the impulse for sugar.

I'm proud of my body and who I am. I was persecuted online when I came into this field, teaching self-love, working with people on their centralism, their sexualism, their intimate relationship. I had radio shows about sex and positions. I was branded the passion news. One woman harassed me twice. She said, "You think you're so beautiful? Are you trying to get every man to look at you?" I wanted to write, "Honey, I already got it now." That would have been bitching, so I said, "I want you ladies to kill this too."

I also understand that we're all the image and likeness of God, the perfect reflection. Humanity sees you as God sees you. They are going to see you in your divine light. You don't have to still feel insecure and worried.

Build your strength into that space of fear, and remember there is no saber-toothed tiger out to eat us or big fat woolly mammoth wanting to slap us around. We are not going to die if someone rejects us.

If you lose your job, are you going to die? No. Are you going to be homeless? Not if you get another job and do work. Are you going to starve to death? I don't think so. You can get food. Keep building it back like that, and you can take the wind out of fear's sails.

HOW DO YOU TAP INTO YOUR DIVINE FEMININE AND WILD SIDE EACH DAY?

Allow the divinity in your life every moment. You're here as an infinite spiritual being in a human body, with a beautiful mind, body, and spirit.

We are powerful women and men. Step into your boots of power because you were meant to be here. You have a divine purpose. Get out of just the human and allow the grace of Spirit to come through you, and you will know what you were meant to do.

Do you want to evolve? Do you want to live your life to the fullest? If so, it's just a mental switch.

My mental switch burned out, from PTSD from childhood trauma from that accident. I was going to die, and I could not function until I kicked my saboteur to the curb and said no. I finally saw who I am in this lifetime. From then on, I never looked back.

If you were dying and you had children, you would probably do something, so do it now. Whatever your story is, there's a way out, a way to the other side.

It starts with the curiosity of playing with the universe to create greatness. That's how I create--how I manifest homes, how I have the greatest love affairs. By the greatest love affair, I don't necessarily mean sex. That is beautiful. It means the greatest interconnected relationships with humanity.

I have emotional love affairs with women, and I'm straight. I have the most interconnected relationships with men, sexual or non-sexual.

It's about the essences, the graces, the beauty, the centralism of who you are. You deserve to be a wild woman because you're freaking fantastic, and it's your divine right.

DUALITY DARE

Alchemy

Alchemy is the process of taking something ordinary and turning it into something extraordinary, sometimes in an unexplainable way. This is how I experience Mia. She transmutes disease, pain, injury and darkness into growth, beauty, love and self-acceptance.

When I think about alchemy, I think of miracles. I believe that when we create space for miracles to happen in our lives, and we believe in our own ability to alchemize, we can begin to transmute any darkness into light. Some might call this magic. I call it the power of the divine feminine.

I remember my first experience with alchemy. After I lost my baby during pregnancy, I went into a deep depression. It was honestly the deepest well of darkness I've ever seen.

I decided to go on a transformational journey during a ten-day silent meditation retreat. During this retreat, I created space for myself. I Asked Creator, God, Universe, the Divine to give me the tools to create space for love and light again. I asked that my body be healed to create light out of the darkness and the grief that plagued me.

I felt the connection in my bones and my body, and more specifically my solar plexus. I literally felt this dark churning bundle of pain centered inside me and spiraling out of control. I opened myself up to possibility, to use this pain to transmute the darkness and give birth to the light.

And pure light was born. Three months later, I discovered I was pregnant with my daughter Lainee (after one too many whiskeys at a Cowboy Bar in Southern Colorado with my ex-husband).

For your Duality Dare, think about what miracles in your life have been birthed from darkness. Write down three ways light came from darkness in your life.

Now how were you responsible for that alchemy? What choices did you get to make to create, transmute and rebirth something beautiful out of pain and adversity?

Use this "mad lib":

I am an alchemist. This adversity _____ ____was transmuted into this _____ miracle.

CHAPTER 22

CHOICE
LAURA SCHAKOSKY

Laura Schakosky is a soul therapy business coach, but she's also known as a celebrity makeup artist and online educator. Laura has worked with future fortune 500 companies and thousands of celebrities, including Elizabeth Taylor, Nicole Kidman, and Elle Macpherson.

I started out in Dallas, Texas as an entrepreneur. I was inspired by Forbes magazine and entrepreneurs. My ultimate goal was to be on the cover of those magazines, but I kept saying I'd do it later.

I became a makeup artist and worked with the stars to get to know people one on one. I wanted to learn what makes these people tick. What is the psychology behind these big, successful people? What's their mindset? How do they relate to other people?

That took me out to Hollywood, and eventually, into a transformational journey that changed my life. Through the experiences I had, now I get to help people see the whole picture from the inside out, and then how to shine online.

Many people have a vision, but they don't have the tools to get there. What I've learned along the way is that you have to clear your energy on every single level, and step into your power on every level. It's a balancing act.

If we're stuck in the past, and we're not dealing with our past, we can't be present to the power we have now to be able to fully share gifts.

That's what I'm working on now. I coach people and help them to clear the path, then give them the tools to be online powerfully, from image to mindset to everything.

HOW DO YOU DEFINE A MODERN WOMAN?

Today we're taught that you graduate high school, go to college, get married, and have kids, because you don't have that much time to have kids.

I think the modern woman says, wait a minute, I can be my own boss, call the shots, and I can take the lid off. I can make as much money as I want to make.

Many people have kids later on in life. They're freezing their eggs or adopting. They want to know who they are before they get into a long-term relationship.

I think a lot of women know that once they get married and have kids, all our energy will go more towards the children as they're growing up, or nurturing the husband and the relationship. Somehow, somewhere, people get lost in all of that.

The modern woman, I believe, is somebody who says no, I need to know myself first. How can I be powerful in the world if I don't know who I am?

She's also someone who understands she is the one generating the way her life looks. Everything we're thinking and believing about ourselves in the world is true.

I think that's a really important thing to be aware of. We have to go back to being conscious if we want to create something big. Our thoughts give us the ability to do what we want to do or not.

IN WHAT AREAS OF YOUR LIFE HAVE YOU STEPPED OUT OF CULTURAL NORMS, DEFIED THEM, OR GONE AGAINST THEM? AND IN THOSE AREAS OF YOUR LIFE WHERE YOU'VE DONE THAT, HAVE YOU EXPERIENCED ANY SHAME OR GUILT, EITHER EXTERNAL OR INTERNAL? IF SO, HOW DID YOU MANAGE THAT?

The biggest breakthrough I ever had was when my mother said, "You need to go to college, you need to get a job, you need to create stability for your life," all that stuff, and I thought, you know what? I don't think that's my path?

There I was in the middle of going to school to become a psychologist, and my makeup career took off. I decided, "I need to do this now."

Breaking that pattern of doing what has always been done was one of the biggest ways I stepped outside cultural norms.

My dad did not get a college degree. My dad is a multimillionaire. He's in the oil business, and he's done extremely well.

My mom doesn't have a college degree, either. She worked her way up and has had her own million-dollar business in the grocery industry.

I've always had examples that if you have your mind set to what you want, you can accomplish anything. I think those role models helped me.

I kind of feel like everything in life is chocolate or vanilla. We choose chocolate because we choose chocolate or we choose vanilla because we choose vanilla. That's just a metaphor, but once we have a choice, the path lays out. We start to learn something powerful about ourselves. There's no shame or guilt around that. It's just a journey.

HOW DO YOU TAP INTO YOUR DIVINE FEMININE AND WILD SIDE EACH DAY?

A lot of it has to do with meditation, including setting up the space. I call it my creative incubator. I bought an infrared sauna that has color therapy, sound therapy and aromatherapy. It's my space to go into these deep meditative states and shamanic journeys to the heart so that I can access that part of myself.

When I do that, it sets my spirit free, because when I'm in that place of pure authenticity, it shows up in the world. When I go and do sessions with people and take them on these magical journeys, I've already fueled myself, so I'm not giving and don't have any energy left for me.

I also do Kundalini Yoga. It opens up all the chakras and the energy, and it makes your creativity soar. Every time I'm going to exercise, I'm going to ask a question, and then I'm going to do a workout, and my body will be relaxed. And the answer will appear, not only in meditation, but I'm going to look all over my life to see how it's going to show up.

I firmly believe we have all the answers inside of ourselves. We have that wild, spirited part of ourselves that's there. We just have to ask questions and focus on it, and then it'll show up everywhere.

I also do mirror work. You go to the mirror every morning while you're getting ready and say, where is it I'm supposed to make the most difference for people? Then listen to yourself, because that's where the answers are. Listen, then act immediately on those inspirations.

DUALITY DARE

Choice

The modern woman is faced with lots of choices. We fought for our choices, we fought for our sovereignty, we fought for the ability to vote, and we fought for our rights.

To some degree, we're still fighting for our choices. If we choose one thing, sometimes the path that's laid out doesn't give us a lot of room to choose both.

It's very difficult to have it all, all at once. I think we can have it all for different seasons. My mom used to say we can have everything we want in life, just not everything at the same time.

I like to think everything is possible for modern day women. But I also know that it comes with a lot of different and new challenges.

Sometimes I wonder if I would have even built the companies I built had I not, as a young woman in my twenties, been a single mom...had I not had the deep why of caring for my daughter.

I know that only part of my success was to ensure that my daughter was cared for. Part of my drive and resilience lived inside of her, yet at the same time lived inside of me.

For your Duality Dare, identify a choice you've been able to make in your life as a modern woman that our great grandmothers were not able to make? What choice have you made that has been most defining in your life?

Play the "what if" game. What if you made the exact opposite choice in that defining moment? Take a moment to map that out, then reflect. In what ways did your defining choice serve you, and in what ways has it possibly hindered you?

What can you learn from this "what if" game? What if you are one choice away from a new path, journey or outcome? Can you see that you are leading your life by the choices you make, and you are currently one choice away from redefining yourself and your life if you choose to do so?

CHAPTER 23

MONKEYS
LAUREN CLAIRE

Lauren Claire is a multi-passionate entrepreneur who helps other creative entrepreneurs bring forward their true voice, their true self, and show up authentically online, so they can create money on their terms.

I've always known there's more to life than the typical nine to five job and living in a house, which wasn't my biggest goal. My biggest goal was location independence.

I was very up for traveling full time, so I traveled from late 2016 right up until 2019.

I've done the standard thing where you go home, you'd save all your money, you'd work multiple jobs, and then you would go traveling and live the best life you've ever had.

It reached a point where I couldn't keep doing that. I couldn't keep going home and working and then coming back out to travel.

I've always known that the online realm was for me; I just didn't know where I fit in. First, I landed in virtual assisting. I found one of those adverts that you always get on Facebook, and I signed up for a course and became a VA. It was amazing. I was making money on my own terms. I was traveling the world.

But it just didn't feel right. It didn't feel aligned. I was working behind the scenes, instead of being the face of my business.

I wanted to be the face of my own business. I want to inspire and empower people to take action and build their own businesses. Making that change was scary and expensive, but I went ahead and did it anyway.

I've pivoted all the way along the way. Today I'm a business and confidence coach, and I wouldn't have it any other way.

HOW DO YOU DEFINE A MODERN WOMAN?

I think of words like super woman or superpowers, in the sense that you can achieve anything. You can be anyone you want to be, and you don't have to feel guilty about it. Frequently we do, and stop ourselves from doing what we want to do. I've been there, I've done that. I've tried to squeeze myself into the mold of somebody else, or what somebody expected me to be, and it just didn't fit.

I went down the corporate road of wanting to look great, wear the clothes, and wear the heels. If anybody's watched Suits on Netflix, that's what I was aspiring to be like--working in this huge law firm.

I got there. I even had a boyfriend who worked in the corporate world with me. I was doing all the right things. And I've never felt more uncomfortable in my entire life. I ended up just quitting. I quit my boyfriend, my family, my job, my life, and moved to South Africa.

I spent a year in a sanctuary in South Africa, working with monkeys and wild animals. All my priorities went into managing the volunteers and looking after these sick animals. It's what I needed to do to get back to myself.

I know the thought of making a bold change scares a lot of people. I would just say, think about yourself first--not from a selfish perspective, from the view of, you are capable of doing anything you want. Do what's best for you before anybody else. Otherwise, people aren't getting your best self, and it's a disservice to everything you're trying to achieve.

IN WHAT AREAS OF YOUR LIFE HAVE YOU STEPPED OUT OF CULTURAL NORMS, DEFIED THEM, OR GONE AGAINST THEM? AND IN THOSE AREAS OF YOUR LIFE WHERE YOU'VE DONE THAT, HAVE YOU EXPERIENCED ANY SHAME OR GUILT, EITHER EXTERNAL OR INTERNAL? IF SO, HOW DID YOU MANAGE THAT?

Definitely evolving what I do in my business. At the end of the day, your people are your people in the online space, and they will follow you, no matter what it is you do. If they truly do believe in you, they want you to be happy.

I tried creating programs and structuring my business in a way I'd seen other people do, and it wasn't working for me. Finally, I said no, I'm not going down this route. This isn't for me. I was scared to evolve and pivot, but I'm all about breaking those boundaries and barriers within the online space.

If I can go out my own way, if it fails the first time or the second time, so what? I'm doing it because I enjoy it, and I'm doing it because it's aligned and it lights me up.

During the really low point of my life, the only way I could think about coming back from that was getting away from the norms of my life. It was very scary for me. Definitely outside my comfort zone.

Once you start doing the uncomfortable stuff, and the more you do it, the easier it becomes to say yes to opportunities you may not have said yes to even a couple of months ago.

Go after what makes you happy, what lights you up, what feels right to you. Even if you're in a bad or sticky situation right now, there's light at the end of the tunnel. There's something else out there--

131

something that could spiral your entire life into the path that you're truly meant to be on.

HOW DO YOU TAP INTO YOUR DIVINE FEMININE AND WILD SIDE EACH DAY?

I think it's always there for me. It's never not there. Even if I'm doing something as simple as cleaning the house, I feel that energy around me.

Many people say to me, "You're just such a positive person, and you've always got a good outlook on life," which I don't think I do. But I always try and just look for the good in everything. The cup is half full, not half empty, for me. I'm always trying to bring people up.

Not going to lie, I get most creative when I've had a drink and I'm sitting down. I had to go into the office in my corporate job and then go for a lunch break. If it was a Friday, I wanted to have a drink with friends, but I couldn't.

Now I do get to sit down with my job and a glass of wine or champagne, and I write. Writing brings me leads, brings me clients, and brings me joy.

The norm of life for most people is to get up, go to work, and don't break any of the rules, whereas I'm here breaking all the rules. I'm sitting on my couch, in sweatpants, drinking wine.

There are many different ways to do life. Tap into that. Don't think about the yes or the no, or the right or the wrong. There are so many different ways of living as yourself.

DUALITY DARE

Monkeys

The tipping point for some of us can be random, unexpected, and a bit odd. My tipping point was not going to South Africa and working

132

at a sanctuary with monkeys, like it was for Lauren, but I definitely had one.

It's that moment in time where you realize that life is too short to be going down this b***s*** path laid out before us in this computer-programmed way. It's like we're all expected to keep going through the day-to-day routines on autopilot, without much thought or intention behind what we do. We go to our 9 to 5, we come home, we order Dominos, watch Netflix, collect retirement, and die.

No thanks.

What's it going to take to shake up your routine and shake up your purpose? As modern women, we get to explore the duality here. What if you take a moment and explore the possibility of doing everything the opposite of what you've been told to do?

Has there been a tipping point, like there was for Lauren, in your life? Can you pinpoint an area of your life where you just couldn't take it anymore? Where a circumstance or situation came up to give you the resolve to make changes?

Maybe it hasn't happened yet. Sometimes people need to fall face-first on the cement to create the next level of their life. Sometimes you need to take a plane to South Africa and work with monkeys to get kicked back into a different perspective. Sometimes we just need to change the angle and enroll another person with a fresh perspective and set of eyes to show us another way.

Your Duality Dare today is to do the opposite of at least ten things you normally do. Yep--ten. You decide. I'm not asking you to call in sick for work (although you can if you want!), but I am daring you to be curious. If you always wake up and have coffee, have tea. If you go to the gym, go on a run. If you always eat a green smoothie, eat a donut. (I can hear the gasps now!)

Go for it. Change the angle and be curious, just like Curious George. (Maybe Lauren and her monkeys are on to something.)

CHAPTER 24

OVERACHIEVER
MARTA SPIRK

Marta Spirk is an empowerment coach, speaker, writer, and podcaster, who helps women move past perfectionism, imposter syndrome, and comparison and into visibility, credibility and profit.

I'm originally from Brazil. My entrepreneurial journey started at age fourteen, when I began teaching English getting paid for it. I tutored people in my home or went to their homes.

I went on to get a bachelor's and a master's in linguistics and languages. I still work as an interpreter for Colorado courts where I live.

In 2016, I had triplets, and it sent me on a soul searching journey of asking, what am I doing with my life? What am I leaving behind? What am I teaching these kids? What is my purpose, and especially with the pressure of three kids at the same time?

No do-over opportunity. No learning from experience and will do better next time. It's just all at the same time.

That's when I found this desire in my heart to share the feelings and the struggles, because lots of people look at me as this super human person. I'm not. In this journey, I shared my struggles and my vulnerability, and say, if I can do it, anyone can.

As I shared this journey, I noticed lots of women were interested in understanding more. It evolved into empowering and helping women entrepreneurs, because most of us are moms juggling all the things and having all these desires, and being shamed for having these desires.

HOW DO YOU DEFINE A MODERN WOMAN?

I talk a lot about being empowered, which means different things for different people. It means taking responsibility for your life, taking responsibility for your happiness, taking responsibility for your success.

I'm an achiever, and for the longest time, I thought it was why I had all these desires. I thought it was why I couldn't settle for just " being a mom" and just staying with the triplets, and letting that be that. I thought it was about my personality.

Working with women entrepreneurs for the last few years, I noticed they are high achieving regardless of their personality type. It's almost like we're addicted to feeling overwhelmed, because we want to do all the things simultaneously. On the one hand, that's great, because others don't even permit themselves to go after these things. It's also a lot of pressure, and we end up putting our worth on the things we do.

Go after what you want. Understand it's yours for the taking. Don't blame the economy, don't blame your spouse for lack of support, don't blame your family, don't blame your audience that is not interested. Understand that if you want it, you go for it.

But also understand how important it is to honor your energy and health, because much like a mom that can't pour from an empty cup, an entrepreneur cannot serve if they are not taking care of themselves. So, it's honoring those two sides.

IN WHAT AREAS OF YOUR LIFE HAVE YOU STEPPED OUT OF CULTURAL NORMS, DEFIED THEM, OR GONE AGAINST THEM? AND IN THOSE AREAS OF YOUR LIFE WHERE YOU'VE DONE THAT, HAVE YOU EXPERIENCED ANY SHAME OR GUILT, EITHER EXTERNAL OR INTERNAL? IF SO, HOW DID YOU MANAGE THAT?

For a long time, I thought I needed to explain myself anytime I felt criticized. When I realized I didn't have to explain any of it, and that the people that get it will get it, it's like the waters parted. There's freedom in realizing you don't need to prove yourself to anybody.

Some people spend their entire lives running away from who they are, because they're trying to belong. I've done that, too, so my goal is to help women stop running away from themselves, and instead take the time to look. And then love and accept what you see.

There will be people who won't accept and love, and will still judge, but it won't feel the same. It won't be as hurtful or offensive because you start seeing that everyone has their own lens.

They're entitled not to like who you are, and to not agree with who you are. It's your job, at all times, to agree with and accept who you are.

Take an observer stance to who you are, and understand that you are not your thoughts. Then actively pay close attention to what you're thinking, what you're feeling, how you're reacting.

Whenever those moments hit, and you're feeling depressed, for example, and there's no reason, dig through that. You'll find the reason, such as, "Oh, I saw that one post, and I compared myself."

Start paying attention to what you're saying--not only vocally, but what you're saying in your head.

HOW DO YOU TAP INTO YOUR DIVINE FEMININE AND WILD SIDE EACH DAY?

I like to say there are usually two camps of people. First, they are doing too much, and that's why they don't see a lot of results. They're overwhelmed, and they don't allow themselves to take a step back and analyze what's working and what isn't.

Then there's the camp that's doing too little. People don't know they exist, because they're hiding behind that perfectionism, that imposter syndrome, that comparison.

Depending on where you stand, it's really finding the balance between the two. For me, because I'm such a doer, my goal is to be able to take a step back, breathe, and reassess.

But then there's the temptation of, I'm not even going to do anything. If I can't do everything, I'm just going to sit here, in depressed mode, with Netflix and ice cream. This is what happens. We burn out and say screw it, I'm closing up shop. Isn't that the indication you're taking things too far?

For some people, they're not doing a whole lot because they always stop themselves. A lot of the overwhelm is just their thoughts, not their actions. It's being able to take that step back as well, so you can step into action.

For me, what helps is taking action when I'm not naturally taking action, because I always do. It's permitting myself to enjoy the lull, which is hard because I'm not producing.

When I permit myself to accept that there will be a lull, but there will also be middles, it encourages me to take action again. I don't have to be on a high all the time.

DUALITY DARE

Overachiever

Addiction is real and is not limited to mind-altering drugs, alcohol, or even food. There are many types of addictions. Addiction to me means that you don't know life without it. It becomes the first and last thing you think about day in and day out. It's an autopilot system that cannot be stopped without massive intervention.

The question we want to ask ourselves is, what's underneath this addiction? For a lot of women living in this masculine, high-achieving role we've taken on as modern women, it's performance. It's overachieving, checking the boxes, and hustling. Overachieving is just as dangerous and addictive as anything else our minds can take hold of and run with.

Becoming aware of the underlying reasons as to why you're performing, why you're overachieving, why you're putting so much pressure on yourself to do and to be "perfect," is how we shift, avoid burnout and remember the divine feminine.

Overwhelm, stress, and anxiety wreak havoc on your health, relationships, business, family, and overall life. How do we take a step back and slow down? How do we find stillness, ease, and flow within a system that acknowledges and gives accolades to the high performer, the overachiever, the stretched-out business owner who's applauded for ignoring self care?

In this book and on my website www.thedualityofthemodern woman.com/gift there are many ways we could step into the divine feminine. But today, I want you to use this Duality Dare to step into stillness. Permit yourself to do nothing, to be still, to just simply BE. If you need permission from outside yourself, I'm giving it to you now.

Step one: Permission. Say this out loud: I permit myself to be still for fifteen minutes.

Step two: Awareness. Write down one thing that could prevent you from being still. What is giving you anxiety that you will need to set aside for fifteen minutes?

Step 3: Acknowledge. Hug yourself. Yes, I mean it! Reward yourself for creating more ease. Wrap your arms around yourself and say, "You are enough just as you BE."

HOLLYWOOD
MARY BETH RAMSEY

Mary Beth Ramsey is a transformational life coach who helps women transform their lives through transforming their closets. Mary Beth has been a celebrity stylist for over twenty-five years, working with movie stars, actors, and actresses to bring about their image to connect with their audience and really step into their success and power.

I moved to Los Angeles about twenty-five years ago and immediately started working with actors on TV shows and movies.

I didn't even think twice about it. I just moved. It was very different from anyone I knew at the time. Nobody in my little Northern California town moved away to do something like this. Everyone was getting married and having children.

I have a background in sewing and clothing. I've been sewing since I was five. With my training, I've been working with the script. Most stylists dress people in fashion. What's new, what's hip, what's now?

What I do is dress people for their character, and their character's development within the story. I start with who they are now, at the beginning of the movie or the story, and seeing their development as a character throughout the movie. I'm showing that in their clothing.

To do this successfully, for yourself, you really have to look into who you are and what your personality is. If you're a business woman and you feel like you need to wear a suit, but you don't feel comfortable wearing a suit, you're not going to come across as who you are. You're not going to attract the right clients to you.

HOW DO YOU DEFINE A MODERN WOMAN?

We're all so different and have so many sides to us, like om, wife, mother, daughter, sister. Then you go into the professional world, and we're also business owners or employees, or co-workers or bosses or managers. Blending that all together is really the modern woman. In the past it was just mom, which is a big job in itself, but now we're taking on these other roles.

When I moved to L.A. to work with celebrities, and worked all those hours, it really limited dating and family life. There are people in this world who are married and have families, but it's rare because of the hours we work.

Do you want to have a family, but then have someone else raise your kids because you work eighteen hours a day and never see them?

This balancing act goes along with people who do have families, and even with people who have animals as their family, it's still hard for them to find the time and the balance.

I was raised in a small town, with everyone asking, whom are you dating? When are you going to get married? Is he the one? Our whole lives as women, we hear that. Part of me had that in me.

But I trusted my instinct that it was time. I had to go. And the jobs I wanted just fell into place. When it falls into place like that, it means you're in the right place. You're going where you're supposed to go.

IN WHAT AREAS OF YOUR LIFE HAVE YOU STEPPED OUT OF CULTURAL NORMS, DEFIED THEM, OR GONE AGAINST THEM? AND IN THOSE AREAS OF YOUR LIFE WHERE YOU'VE DONE THAT, HAVE YOU EXPERIENCED ANY SHAME OR GUILT, EITHER EXTERNAL OR INTERNAL? IF SO, HOW DID YOU MANAGE THAT?

It's funny because when I moved to L.A., all my friends were married with children, so that's what they're talking about. I was so different. I had no clue about any of that stuff.

Most of my friends in L.A. are single with no kids, so we talk about work and going out for dinner and vacations. It's completely different conversations.

I was married at one point, and I was a stepmom. During that time, if I wasn't working, I was more involved with the school. I would take the kids to school, and I would volunteer.

I'd start talking about family stuff, but I felt like my comments and questions were stupid, because the kids were already elementary school age. It would have been different if I had raised them from the beginning as a stay-at-home mom, but I didn't. I did feel like other moms looked down on me for not knowing certain things.

In Hollywood, you don't know when a freelance job is going to come. Sometimes, I'd have three months off or one week off. Switching back and forth is difficult, as in going and making money and being a worker and a boss or whatever, and then switching into the feminine and being at home.

I would come home and immediately kind of step into the wife and mother, and think, how come the kitchen is dirty? I haven't been home for 18 hours, of course, it's dirty. But why didn't they clean it? Because they don't think that way.

143

There were lots of frustrations, and here I am being masculine at work and coming home and trying to be feminine, but not really being able to, because of the dynamic at home.

HOW DO YOU TAP INTO YOUR DIVINE FEMININE AND WILD SIDE EACH DAY?

When I'm heavy into my work and being the boss, and doing the paperwork and delegating, it's a very masculine role, and I get things done. When I do that too much without a break, I break down.

We women are naturally receivers, nurturers, instead of bosses. Having so much masculinity in my life that I was dealing with, I had to cry and let it out.

It's sexist, in a way, to say we like to shop, and that we want to do our hair and our makeup and nails. But we need to relax into being a woman, so then we can be masculine. We need both.

Shopping nurtures me, even if I'm not spending money. I love walking up and down the street and looking at beautiful things in the windows.

It's just getting back in touch with what makes us tick and what makes us happy. Whether it's laying on the beach or reading a book or laying in the bathtub, or putting on makeup just for ourselves, or whatever we do to nurture ourselves.

Go back to when you were a teenager or a kid, and figure out who you were. What did you like to do? Do you still like to do it? What do you like to do now?

How can you bring that into your life and still have a day off? Or have a couple of hours off each day to get back to who you are.

If we feel beautiful, that energy will come out, and we are beautiful. When we feel beautiful, we get more done. We just take control. We feel powerful in our beauty.

DUALITY DARE

Hollywood

Shape shifting from a small town girl to dressing Hollywood celebrities to stepmom to single. How do we navigate all the roles? Do we leave parts of us behind to pick up a new identity? How do we decide what parts of us come along for the ride when the seasons of our lives change?

It's important to identify what parts of us are always parts of us, regardless of the season of life we're in. For a lot of women, as we shift from motherhood to empty nesters to retirees, we might feel a little lost along the way.

Rediscovering who we are with each passing season of our lives is important for our own values. So, we can continually feel worthy and confident in whatever season we're in. I believe parts of us get to be left behind because there are parts of us that don't serve us in all seasons of our lives.

There are also parts of us that do serve us in all seasons of our lives, whether mothering, running a business, golfing, or in deep with a partner.

In this Duality Dare, I challenge you to look at the different seasons of your life and quantify them into three sections. In each section, write down what ways of BEing you embodied that served your highest good in each season, and what ways of BEing didn't serve your highest good.

For example, if I said single mom season, business growth season, teenage mom season, the ways of being in all three of those seasons were: Committed, loving, and powerful. The ways of BEing that did not serve me in those seasons were: Disconnected, aloof, and scarce.

145

Can we release the ways of BEing that are not serving us, and continue to align with the ways of BEing that serve in every season of our lives?

What are you going to release that is no longer serving you, regardless of the season that you're in? Write it down in your journal and declare that this way of being no longer serves you.

Duality Dare Exercise

1. Identify three seasons of your life: _____
    ._____ _____

2. Write down three ways of BEing that served you in all the seasons.

3. Write down three ways of BEing that did not serve you in all three seasons.

4. What are you willing to let go of in the next season of your life so you can fully embody the ways of BEing that support you?

5. Say this out loud: I am free of the attachment to _____ (what you are letting go of) so I can fully embody the ways of BEing that are for my highest good.

CHAPTER 26

REBEL
SUSAN SAINT-ROSSY

Susan Saint-Rossy has been a relationship expert for over 20 years. She specializes in and mentors couples where women make more money than the man in the relationship.

I'm going to start with why I moved directly out of being a general relationship therapist to doing this more specific work with entrepreneurial women. It goes back a long time because I am sixty-seven years old. I have been a college professor and a Marketing Director for a very large, international consulting firm.

In my late thirties, I went back to school to get a degree in clinical social work to do therapy. I've lived worldwide while following my husband, who was a diplomat for many years. I reached a point where something clicked inside me, and I realized I needed something to do that was more creative.

This has happened throughout my life, where I've wanted something more creative. I was not feeling right about being constrained by the structure of therapy. I became interested in the online world and what was happening among women as entrepreneurs.

That took me to this very creative, wonderful world. I love working with women CEOs and those trying to balance their big careers and businesses with having a loving relationship and a family.

HOW DO YOU DEFINE A MODERN WOMAN?

It's a woman who's taking the best of feminism, using the women's rights that we've gotten in the last fifty years to do exactly what she wants to do, and being creative in doing that.

She's out there doing something in the world, making an impact in any way that she desires, but at the same time, is taking care of her family, and having a balanced relationship between that work and her relationship with her partner (and kids, if she has kids).

I think it's important for women today to understand they have this basis from which to become more and move more away from patriarchy--away from the old white man making the decisions--to having power, developing wealth, and making a difference in the world.

The biggest struggle I see with women making their own mark on the world is that they put on their CEO hat and take on a deep responsibility to build a business, take care of their employees, and make decisions all day long. In a way, it's very masculine energy.

When I still worked in an office, and knew I was coming home to my three kids and my husband, I would drive around town, listening to a book on tape, usually fiction, where I could just be in fantasy for a little while. Then I'd pull into my garage, having released my workday, so I could meet my family in a way that felt good to me.

Now I dance around the room before I go out. Anything that changes your brain or focuses on that rational, logical thinking into the intuitive, creative zone.

IN WHAT AREAS OF YOUR LIFE HAVE YOU STEPPED OUT OF CULTURAL NORMS, DEFIED THEM, OR GONE AGAINST THEM? AND IN THOSE AREAS OF YOUR LIFE WHERE YOU'VE DONE THAT, HAVE YOU EXPERIENCED ANY SHAME OR GUILT, EITHER EXTERNAL OR INTERNAL? IF SO, HOW DID YOU MANAGE THAT?

I've been a rebel since birth. Yes, I got a Ph.D. in English because my family is a bunch of teachers. I thought it was expected of me. I got a tenure track job. After two years, I realized I didn't want to be a scholar.

Next, I went to corporate America, got a job in a consulting firm, and worked there for a few years. Then I realized I didn't like what I was doing there, so I got them to give me a more creative role. That still wasn't me, so I rebelled again by returning to school and getting my master's in social work to become a therapist. That was where my spirit and my heart wanted to go.

One of the most out of the ordinary things I have done was getting married when I was forty-six to a man I didn't really know that well, and who was getting ready to go to China.

I married him and we went to China, leaving everybody behind. I had my first baby at age forty-nine. At age fifty-five, after we'd been to Russia, then Botswana in Southern Africa, I had twins.

I sort of felt guilty when I left academia, because I felt like I was disappointing my family. The biggest guilt or shame I felt is around having children so late, and it partly came from inside because of the lifespan. They're not going to be fifty or sixty years old when I die unless I am really, really unusual.

When I was pregnant, some people who knew how old I was shamed me about it. But most people were supportive. Whether they supported me or not, it's my life.

HOW DO YOU TAP INTO YOUR DIVINE FEMININE AND WILD SIDE EACH DAY?

What you're describing, the divine feminine is creativity, or the creative force. I used to teach mythology and the creation myths from pre-Christianity. There was a lot about women and the matriarchy and the goddess.

To me, that's creativity. Creativity is where I connect with that divine feminine, and it's also where I'm my wildest.

I love to paint, and I used to be a dancer. If I don't take the time to do those creative activities, I don't feel like I'm myself.

I try to help my clients with--finding what connects them to that creative force. If things go well, they can find it both in their work and outside of their work, home life, and relationships.

I want people to understand that, yes, there's art, and there are their creative art forms, but creativity is much bigger than that. It's very, very important to me.

DUALITY DARE

Rebel

Susan demonstrates that living life by your own set of rules can be extremely fulfilling, yet also create some fear, bring up shame, and maybe even apprehension over what others think. I believe she demonstrates such a powerful stand for women when it comes to creating your own path.

Susan says in her interview that she's always been a rebel. What does a rebel mean to you? For me, I've always felt like I'm an outlier. To a certain degree, I do things according to the norms, but then I completely take a left turn. I go back and forth. I consider myself a rebel.

I know a lot of us do. Maybe we just need to own that term and redefine it. Create space for yourself to really be rebellious against the norms, cultural restrictions, and restraints put on us.

Today for Duality Dare, I want you to check in with your inner rebel. Do they want you to live like a rebel? What can you do today to rebel against the norms?

Write down three things that make you feel wild, rebellious, and courageous. What if you were bold and audacious today and decided that life would be built around YOUR matrix, not the one designed for you by cultural norms.

Here are a few examples to get you started. If I'm rebellious, I'm going to say no when I'm supposed to say yes. What are the energetic rules in your life that you can break?

Here's a list of rules I've identified that I like to break:

- Don't talk about money, politics, or sex. It's not polite.

- Don't wear anything too short, too low cut, or too tight.

- Don't be too loud.

- Don't ask for what you desire in the bedroom.

- Don't self pleasure.

- Don't air your dirty laundry.

- To be polite, you must always eat what the hostess serves.

Do any of these feel true for you? If so, use them and decide today which one you are going to REBEL against.

If you always stick with small talk, why not rebel, and at your next dinner date, dive into sex, money or politics? If you are not sexually satisfied with your partner in the bedroom, ask for what you want. If you love to show off your legs, wear super short shorts. Rebel and be curious about what you discover.

CHAPTER 27

PONO
MAYAN TRAN

Mayan Tran is a certified NLP practitioner and hypnotherapist specializing in getting to the root of an issue at the subconscious level, so past pain and trauma can be released.

My parents wanted the best for me. They wanted me to go to college. So, I did, and I majored in IT Technology. I had a consulting career for 16 years.

From the beginning, I knew that was not for me, even when I got my internship. But what do you do when this is the path you've gone down? I felt like it was too late for me to start over at forty, which now sounds really silly to think about.

But that's how it felt--going through my life feeling like I was living someone else's life, that someone else had laid out for me. I felt like I was on autopilot. I had the house, the marriage, all the things, but I felt so inauthentic.

Around thirty-three, I started thinking, okay, there's got to be more to my life. I was part of a multi-level marketing company, and from that I started doing personal development. It opened up my eyes to the fact that there's a different way to live that I wasn't taught.

I started re-creating my life and moved to California. In my heart, that was where I needed to be. That one move opened up doors that wouldn't have been possible.

I knew the power of Feng Shui and the power of using the energy of your space to create what you want. At the same time, I recognize that there's no such thing as limitation. I wanted to find out how to help women break out their limiting beliefs around what they wanted and see that we can be independent, be powerful, and create our lives.

HOW DO YOU DEFINE A MODERN WOMAN?

It means I know who I am. I know my truth. I'm in touch with my desires and what is authentically me. I'm in touch with my power. I'm in touch with my strength, and I'm unapologetic about it.

I'm showing up the way I want to show up because it's who I am, not because I'm trying to please somebody or make them feel comfortable. It's feeling that freedom to be yourself, and then knowing who you are, and knowing you have choices in whom you want to be and how you create your life.

The beauty of being a modern woman is the choices we have to create our lives the way we want. There's not just one way of living. We get to choose our own way.

A misconception that goes along with that is, we have to be all the things, all the time. Yes, we have all the choices. We're at a buffet where all the choices are in front of us. But that doesn't mean we need to eat everything on one trip, right?

On my first trip to the buffet table, I can pick out these different things. This is what I want to take in right now. On my next trip, I get to choose different things. It's up to me.

The trap is feeling like you have to do, be, and have everything simultaneously. I think it goes back to the choice. We get to choose what we want to be, do, and have at any given moment. That's the beauty and the challenge.

IN WHAT AREAS OF YOUR LIFE HAVE YOU STEPPED OUT OF CULTURAL NORMS, DEFIED THEM, OR GONE AGAINST THEM? AND IN THOSE AREAS OF YOUR LIFE WHERE YOU'VE DONE THAT, HAVE YOU EXPERIENCED ANY SHAME OR GUILT, EITHER EXTERNAL OR INTERNAL? IF SO, HOW DID YOU MANAGE THAT?

For one, I ended my marriage. I had a lot of internal guilt and shame around that, because we were in a relationship for over eighteen years, and married for twelve of those years. It was no longer working, and we grew apart.

We'd gone to counseling. We'd done all the things, but at the end of the day, I felt like we were better off apart, with other partners who were better for us.

That carried a lot of guilt on my part--guilt of creating pain for other people. For him, and also for our families and friends. There's a lot of pressure in appeasing people and making sure they don't feel the impact of changes you make.

What led me to the decision was knowing myself and being honest about whether this was what my heart and soul were yearning for.

I also had a support system that really encouraged me. I had a coach at the time, I had best friends that I talked to regularly, and they really helped me see that this is my life. I'm Hawaiian, and there's a term called Pono. If you're good, you're Pono. If you're good with yourself, if you're good with your choices, then you can move forward without other people's opinions affecting you.

I don't think I'm alone in experiencing a relationship you've grown out of. It took me a ton of courage and doing my due diligence of going to counseling, to make sure we'd done everything we could do to fix things. After we did that, it was clear in my heart that ending it was the right move.

HOW DO YOU TAP INTO YOUR DIVINE FEMININE AND WILD SIDE EACH DAY?

For me, divine feminine is creative. It's reflective, it's still. It's flowy. I always start my day with meditation and journaling. Journaling is the very first thing I do. I let my mind loose. Whatever needs to come out allows me to start the day off with a fresh, clean slate.

Afterwards I'll do meditation, still my mind, and receive whatever intuitive or spiritual guidance needs to come through. The feminine is also about receiving.

I also like to doodle. Even just doodling in my journal allows me to remain in that mindless space of allowing.

For movement, that usually looks like yoga. Or I'll turn on music if I'm doing my makeup. I move around and shake things off, especially before a coaching call with the client. I'll just shake off the energy.

One of my challenges is allowing myself to be free and loud. Part of that is probably the way I grew up, and part of it is my personality. I'm just not inherently that way.

Being in a partnership with a man who is very much in his masculine creates the space for me to be my crazy feminine. I act a little crazy around him. I can change my mind if I want to about things. It's that dynamic of the feminine and masculine together.

When those two opposite forces are present, the masculine creates the container for the feminine to show up in the wild ways. It's so freeing, being in a space where I can just show up as me, enjoy, and have pleasure in the receiving.

DUALITY DARE

Pono

If you're good with yourself, you're good with your choices, and you're good with what other people think of you. This is what Pono means in Hawaiian. The way Mayan describes this is that, after you're good with what people think of you, you get to protect your Pono with clear boundaries. Boundaries are part of Pono.

I truly feel that boundaries are the highest version of spirituality. Think of it this way; If you set clear boundaries with people, they know what to expect. You're not saying yes when you mean no.

Saying yes when you mean yes also means you're saying yes to being one hundred percent present. It's saying yes to being open to give and receive fully.

If you say yes when you really mean no, you start harboring resentment towards the person and the situation. This creates a disconnect and disharmony--not only for you but for them.

When you're not clear about setting boundaries, and you're saying yes more than you're saying no, you find yourself on a date you really aren't into. You're eating the cake you really don't want to eat at your mother-in-law's party. You agree to go to coffee with an acquaintance that really doesn't make you feel great.

At that point, the question becomes, what do I need from this person pushing me to say yes when I really want to say no? For example, if you continually say yes to someone when you really want to say no, what are you trying to receive from them? Is it acceptance? Love? Support?

For this Duality Dare, list three people you'd like to create boundaries with but always feel compelled to say yes to.

Next, ask yourself this: Why do I keep saying yes to these people? What do I need from them that I'm not getting from myself?

The last step in this Duality Dare is to clearly, firmly and lovingly set a boundary with one of these people in your life today. Go for the Pono.

CHAPTER 28

CATASTROPHIZE
MEGAN FENYOE

Megan Fenyoe is a bestselling author, TEDx speaker, licensed mental health therapist, and the founder of the nonprofit movement I Am Enough.

I've been a mental health therapist for over fifteen years. In 2012, I made this crazy decision, at age thirty-three, to commission as an officer in the Air Force. I wasn't looking for a husband, but sometimes when you're not looking, they appear, and that's what happened. My now ex-husband appeared.

It was a whirlwind relationship. Within eleven months, we were married, and I was living my best life. I was a therapist, and in the Air Force, and just loving life.

Within six months of getting married, things started changing. My ex-husband became increasingly unhappy and angry. I kept catching him in lies. He ended up having an affair for fourteen months of our two-and-a-half-year marriage but blamed me.

Even as a therapist, I did not realize I was involved in such a dysfunctional marriage. It doesn't matter who you are, how old you are, or what you do. Abuse can happen anywhere.

He told me everything was my fault. He was calling me names. I spiraled into a black hole and lost every sense of myself. I didn't think that I wasn't good enough just for him because I catastrophized that story. I decided I wasn't a good therapist, I wasn't a good friend, or a good sister.

In February of 2018, I finally walked away from him. Three months before that, I had lost my six-figure income. I hit rock bottom and had no idea what I was going to do. By the grace of God, I jumped into this entrepreneurship thing. I also got myself into my own therapy and started doing my trauma work. Although heartbreaking and difficult, it's been the most amazing journey.

HOW DO YOU DEFINE A MODERN WOMAN?

I just did my first ever TEDx Talk and talked about what it means to be enough. I tell people now that when I started my trauma journey, the phrase "I am enough" has always kind of been there. I even have it tattooed on my collarbone.

When I started my trauma work, I wrote on a notecard every day why I was enough. My first Evernote card said, I am enough because I got out of bed today. After I hit rock bottom, that was the only thing I believed made me enough--that God picked me up or woke me up and got me out of bed.

The more I repeated that statement, the more I was able to start believing the other statements. As therapists, we call it cognitive restructuring, as in restructuring your brain to believe these statements. Today, I am enough means I unapologetically own who I am.

I teach people to say, "I am enough because." You have to have the word because, and you have to tell yourself why you believe that you're enough. It's powerful to say I am enough, but it's even more powerful to say why. That's where that restructuring comes in your brain, when you remind yourself why you're enough.

One of the words we talk about as therapists is reality testing your thoughts. Anchoring is a great way to test the reality of your thoughts. It's literally asking yourself, "Is this catastrophizing thinking?" When you have that negative thought, are you catastrophizing? It's all about testing the reality of our negative thoughts.

IN WHAT AREAS OF YOUR LIFE HAVE YOU STEPPED OUT OF CULTURAL NORMS, DEFIED THEM, OR GONE AGAINST THEM? AND IN THOSE AREAS OF YOUR LIFE WHERE YOU'VE DONE THAT, HAVE YOU EXPERIENCED ANY SHAME OR GUILT, EITHER EXTERNAL OR INTERNAL? IF SO, HOW DID YOU MANAGE THAT?

I've always been very independent when it comes to my career. I have a learning disability, and my guidance counselor in high school told me I was never going to graduate college. I've defied the odds with that.

I've never wanted children, even though I love children. I love my nieces and nephews. People that see me with kids ask, how could you not want kids? It's just never been a thing for me.

Where I grew up, everyone gets married right after high school. I was the girl that went off to college. I grew up in a Christian home, and everyone went to these Christian colleges. I went to the number one party school in Michigan.

There's also the, "Oh, my gosh, aren't you so lonely because you don't have a man?" There are days where I want to have a man, but I've got my best friend I live with, and I'm doing what I love. For me, that's power. You do have to have something that gives you that power.

For me, if I didn't have this movement and my story, I don't know if it would be as easy for me to say, "Oh, I'm so happy." I'm not happy to be single, but I'm okay being single. It's important to have something you're passionate about so that you can defy the norms of society.

I'm a Christian, and I love Jesus. But I just didn't want to go to a Christian school. I felt like God had more for me and wanted me to explore different cultures and people.

When I was doing my trauma work, that's what I was really working on. I didn't realize any of that until I lost the one thing I thought I loved.

I don't apologize for who I am, even though I'm a hot mess half the time.

HOW DO YOU TAP INTO YOUR DIVINE FEMININE AND WILD SIDE EACH DAY?

With accountability, time management, and boundaries. For me, self-care is so important. Every day we have things we have to do. We've got to get up, we've got to eat, we've got to shower, we've got to deal with the kids, we've got to deal with our partner.

Every single day, you need to have something you want to do. That's where it breaks up the mundane part of life. For me, that means I get up and work out. I was in a horrible car accident a year and a half ago, so I live with chronic pain. It's hard for me to work out, but I still do it because for me, that's my mental well-being. That's my escape.

For accountability, I live with my best friend, and she holds me accountable. She'll say Megan, you're a coach, but you don't always do what you tell your clients. Or she'll say, Megan, it's eight o'clock. You've been on your computer all day.

Now I've got boundaries in place. Friday, Saturday, and Sunday are my days to do what I want. There's this guilt and shame around boundaries, especially for women. This is where the belief of being enough and unapologetically owning who you are comes into play. When you believe you're enough, there's no guilt or shame.

DUALITY DARE

Catastrophize

A word I have a hard time pronouncing is not hard for most of us to utilize in our lives. I coach many women, and the catastrophizing of events in our lives can sometimes get out of control.

Our perspective gets a shift when we zoom out to that thirty-thousand-foot view and see what is actually going on. In the moment, it seems like a catastrophe is happening. The divorce, the bankruptcy, losing a job, etc., but I truly believe everything we go through happens in divine timing, for a greater purpose, and for the greater good.

It's hard to get out of that when you're knee deep in the mud. Sometimes just removing yourself from the catastrophe is enough to move you forward and through it.

Everything is in constant flux and motion, and we generate either forward motion, or we generate backwards motion. Life is constantly evolving, and everything is changing all the time.

Perspective helps you manage everything. How will this event shape you? How will the adversity, trauma or experience pull you forward? Or will you allow it to set you back and into a victim's story? A lot of us live in victimhood. I lived there for a very long time.

Perspective is the answer, so I want you to imagine you're seeing your situation from another person's eyes in this Duality Dare. (And if you really want to get woo woo with me, maybe from another dimension.) What's the worst case scenario? If you break it down, you can see a glimpse of hope in your situation to pull you through it?

For your Duality Dare, write down one event, adversity or situation that you're smack in the middle of right now--one where it feels like your world's falling apart, and you seem unable able to let go of it.

For me, one such situation was when my ex-husband and I experienced bankruptcy during the market crash in the early 2000s. We went from young millionaires to young and broke within a matter of weeks. In the moment, I couldn't see a way out. I felt hopeless, exhausted, and frustrated, like there was no other path for me. Now, of course, I can see a different perspective.

Start with an event you're currently facing, and write it down in the journal section. Ask yourself, "What's the worst thing that could happen?"

Next, ask yourself, "What's the best thing that could come out of this?" (Remember all things are possible all the time.)

Normally the fear we have is about the expectations of other people. The worst case scenario is generally not death or starvation but ego-driven. It's the fear of rejection, disapproval, or not living up to societal expectations.

In my example, I realized bankruptcy wasn't going to kill me. I was not going to starve. What I discovered is that my ego was hurt. I was afraid of being hurt, and afraid of what others would think of me. I was afraid of being a failure. I was afraid I wouldn't look good in front of my peers. I could go on and on.

As I said in an earlier Duality Dare, sometimes it takes falling face down on the concrete to create a tipping point. Sometimes the adversities you face are just tipping points in disguise.

So next time you catastrophize, see if instead you can optimize, and shift into a thirty-thousand-foot view.

CHAPTER 29

DIVINITY
PRIYA LAKHI

Priya Lakhi is a master results coach, hypnotherapist and NLP specialist. She's the founder of Awaken Ananda, which specializes in supporting women to integrate intuition with their intelligence.

I spent fifteen years as a criminal defense lawyer working with clients on death row. I was stuck in the very left brain masculine energy of intelligence. I had this very lawyer mentality, which was, if you can't prove it to me, then it's not true. That's what we're taught as lawyers. We seek evidence, seek truth, and do it through a very linear, logical process.

For years, I spent my life in this left brain of intelligence, which is important. But it's not the tree of life. It's the tree of knowledge.

I kept having these intuitive nudges. I could read energy, and I just thought, "Oh, this is just what makes me a good lawyer." No one teaches us that there's this entire right brain that we don't use, that's more powerful, more filled with truth, and more filled with our divine essence.

I kept ignoring these things, so as the universe does when we're not living in our highest potential, I started getting tests and lessons that were catalysts for change.

My relationship was unhappy. My job no longer fulfilled me. My finances were a disaster. My friends and I were drifting apart.

I started asking questions like, why are we here? What does it all mean? I cannot believe that my existence is eat, work, sleep, die. That cannot be the purpose of this existence.

Eventually, the lessons brought me to my knees. The universe said enough is enough. You've skimmed the surface of your divinity, and now we need to bring you all the way in.

HOW DO YOU DEFINE A MODERN WOMAN?

What it means to me is to go back to my ancient wisdom and knowing. To me, that has nothing to do with technology, with legacy, or the impact I want to make. Those things are not relevant to my soul.

I'm playing a character in this lifetime. Being a modern woman is recognizing the ancient wisdom in my bones, in my DNA, in my blood, in my lineage is my superpower. That is what takes me forward. That is what I'm here to spread. That is what I'm here to embody.

It can make an impact on one person or millions. The goal for me as a modern woman is not to get caught in more doing. It's to remember that in the flow of my BEing, all I want comes to me.

I say this with no judgment, because again, I believe the world is always at the right place at the right time, but the patriarchy, or the masculine energies, have ruled our planet for thousands of years. There's a lot of emphasis on logic and having a formula to follow.

But the feminine energy we carry is energy of knowing without proof. It's an energy of being and accomplishing without hustle. It's the understanding that we need community, not competition. It's the nurturing that comes if you have children, which I don't, but I know I have that instinct with my friends and my family.

165

We have such a diverse skill set as women. Can we trust in the knowing that we will always be okay in all ways? That, to me, is the key to being a modern woman.

IN WHAT AREAS OF YOUR LIFE HAVE YOU STEPPED OUT OF CULTURAL NORMS, DEFIED THEM, OR GONE AGAINST THEM? AND IN THOSE AREAS OF YOUR LIFE WHERE YOU'VE DONE THAT, HAVE YOU EXPERIENCED ANY SHAME OR GUILT, EITHER EXTERNAL OR INTERNAL? IF SO, HOW DID YOU MANAGE THAT?

By realizing that we're actually on the planet for learning. We're not here for happiness, which is an entirely interesting concept. We are forced as women to believe in this undeniable standard of having it all.

If you believe the cosmic laws, having it all on this planet means having all the learnings, all the chaos, all the catalysts. Because it is in those moments, we are at a choice point, whether that's one hundred times a day or one hundred times a year.

Do I choose to believe in the power of who I am? In truth? Or do I choose to believe the bullshit stories and lies I have told myself about my insecurities, my fears, and my inabilities?

I allow for the divinity in me to come through and awaken the divinity in somebody else. Doing that generally starts with awareness. What is divinity? What is soul? What is intuition? What is the cosmos? What is ascension? It starts in the mind; it starts with understanding concepts.

It also starts with just an awakening process, but this is after we've done the personal development and healing work. Unless we clear our lower three chakras, which is about our own power, our worth, and self-love, there's no way we can even get to the place where we understand that we are, in fact, the divinity we're seeking.

166

It has to start there through energy healing. I use hypnosis, spiritual coaching, NLP, and inner child work. All of my work has the underlying silver thread of this is a cosmic journey we're on, this is not just a human journey we're on.

HOW DO YOU TAP INTO YOUR DIVINE FEMININE AND WILD SIDE EACH DAY?

Remember that always, in all ways, I will be okay. Within each of us lies all the wisdom, answers, tools, strategies, and solutions. All of these things that we keep looking for on the outside are already within us.

We can make the choice. It's an awareness, an acknowledgement that there is something in my life that isn't working. The first step is to know thyself. Understand, look at it in the mirror, take the time to check in, and say, "Do I have a life that I love? And if I don't, what's not there or what's there that I no longer need?"

After you know yourself, there has to be an acceptance of yourself. Accept without judgment the patterns I've created, the stories I've told myself, the belief systems other people have entrenched in me about what success looks like. Then start questioning everything.

Each of us starts in victimhood. This is not unique to me. We each start this journey in victimhood, which is the belief that life is happening to us. From there, we go to personal empowerment, then soul realization. Only from soul realization can we get to the next step, which is surrender. I trust now not that the world is happening to me, but rather the world is happening for me.

After surrender, we get to something called God realization, which is that I am god. I am the creator. No man is sitting up there in judgment of me.

I don't want to know how to be a better human. I'm interested in understanding my divinity and how to bring that forth through my human form.

DUALITY DARE

Divinity

Soul ascension. Universe. Creator. God. Dharma. Kharma. Cosmos. Spirit. Awakening.

How do these words make you feel? What comes up for you? Be aware right now of how you feel in your body.

I used to feel overwhelmed by these concepts because I thought they were esoteric and only for the enlightened.

Through my own journey, I continue to ask questions, to be curious about these concepts (and many more).

Divinity to me may be different than what it is for you, or your family, or Priya. I want to encourage non-attachment to the words and instead embody a feeling--a knowing--and cultivate your own understanding in this Duality Dare.

The dictionary version uses DIVINE and as an adjective: of, from, or God-like. Therefore you could say that DIVINITY is the state of being God-like.

This is a big topic and one that is very personal, but I want to open something here for you.

Instead of formulating a written personal definition of what divinity is for you, I have a different take on this for you. Put this book down. Place your hands over your heart and feel into your body. Take five deep, slow breaths.

As you say each phrase out loud, make a mental note of how your body responds (if it does), and how it made you feel. Did you feel pulled towards the statement, or did you pull away from the statement? If you aren't sure, try giving your responses a number.

1 is you feel a positive response.

2 is you feel a negative response.

With your hand over your heart, say these phrases out loud and record your mental number or how your body responds.

I am creator.

I am love.

I am universe.

I am source.

I am light.

I am divine.

I am God.

I am energy.

I am spirit.

I am awakened.

I am conscious.

As I was exploring and becoming more curious about my own soul's ascension, this exercise helped me connect language to concepts that felt best to me in my body, soul, and bones. Some may disagree, but it helps anchor me to the so-called esoteric concepts to support my own spiritual path with more awareness. Try it out and see how this feels for you.

CHAPTER 30

FEAR
TARA OLDRIDGE

Tara Oldridge is a mom, a wife, and an entrepreneur, and a podcast host who's been featured in Forbes magazine. Tara has created a two-day workshop that she calls Vision to Business, which helps women build an impactful and profitable business.

There's an auctioneer story people tell about me that illustrates why I don't believe you can ever "get over" fear.

On the first day of a conference I attended, a person on stage said, "I'm going to auction off my boots tomorrow." And I thought to myself, "No, you're not. I'm going to, because I'm an auctioneer." I even wrote down "auction off boots."

I went to sleep that night with butterflies in my stomach because I know the power I have inside me to manifest what I know and see. I already knew it was happening.

The next day she said okay, I don't know what I'm doing. I'm not an auctioneer. That's when I took my moment. I didn't allow her to invite me to the stage because I was already on my way up, butterflies in my stomach or not.

Not only don't I believe you can get over fear, but I also don't believe you should even want to get over it.

It's there whether you choose to tap into it to work against you, or you tap into it to work for you is up to you.

I use fear to catapult me. It's always there. I'm always scared shitless. I've just reframed what that energy means to me. I don't make it bad, or this thing I need to avoid. I think, "Sweet, I'm scared. This is awesome."

Our job isn't to know. It's to have faith.

HOW DO YOU DEFINE A MODERN WOMAN?

I love this question so much, because it's reminding me of why I'm doing what I'm doing. Modern women are rising, though we've got a long way to go.

I would define the modern woman as love. Instead of being a martyr, instead of being a victim, instead of being resentful and bitter of what male society has done to us, we instead look at it as, "Okay, how can we be compassionate for where we've come from?"

How can we be compassionate and take a stand for the vulnerability inside of our men, as opposed to asking, "Well, what can I get? Who can I be, what can I build?"

Instead of trying to be a badass woman, what if we ask, "How can I love?"

It's not about being in demand or being an influencer or being a modern day woman. Let's get back to what matters, by asking, am I being loving?

I have this beautiful business God has given me to lead and link arms with other incredible women. It's not something I feel obligated to do.

I feel very honored and privileged to be creating something that is not of me.

IN WHAT AREAS OF YOUR LIFE HAVE YOU STEPPED OUT OF CULTURAL NORMS, DEFIED THEM, OR GONE AGAINST THEM? AND IN THOSE AREAS OF YOUR LIFE WHERE YOU'VE DONE THAT, HAVE YOU EXPERIENCED ANY SHAME OR GUILT, EITHER EXTERNAL OR INTERNAL? IF SO, HOW DID YOU MANAGE THAT?

Recently I got Botox for the first time, and I cried afterwards, because a lady asked me, "Why? Why are you getting Botox? Why now? What's the reason?" I said, "Well, I don't know. I just kind of feel it's what's next for me. It's a cultural norm."

When I had my daughter, I made this promise I wouldn't do any of that, so I felt like I let myself down. I felt like I let my daughter down. I felt like I let God down.

God says in the Bible, you are fearfully and wonderfully made, and you're created in the image of God. And He doesn't get better than that, right?

Why are we tweaking? Why are we plucking? Why are we syringing? Why are we poking and prodding our bodies? I don't know.

I fell into societal culture, or "not enoughness," if you will. Not gonna lie, I'm probably going to get it done again.

I love the way I'm not perfect. I'm very much married to pieces of earthly and fleshly things. And still, yet I hear God say to me, but I love you. You're so perfect the way you are. Yeah, total shame, total guilt. But not around, "I'm gonna go now and get this Botox." Shame came after the fact.

HOW DO YOU TAP INTO YOUR DIVINE FEMININE AND WILD SIDE EACH DAY?

I do feel really feminine when I do my hair and makeup. I love pairing clothes together, and I love colors. I love pretty things. I desire luxury and love luxury. I love my house to look a certain way. I love beauty.

But when I feel the most feminine, I'm in a childlike state--when I'm goofing around or giggling, or wearing no makeup and a total dorky outfit. I didn't eat, I just threw clothes on, and I'm playing with my horses.

When I feel my most feminine is when I'm not done up. When women are really done up, that feels masculine to me. I don't think that curling your hair and botox and eyelashes and outfits is feminine. I think it's masculine.

In our current society, what we think is beautiful on a magazine cover we also think is feminine. But it's not. It's not enoughness. It's seeking validation. That is not feminine, and I feel most feminine when I'm not wearing makeup.

I never realized how important it is that people see inside of our true authentic lives until I show someone a piece of it.

DUALITY DARE

Fear

Faith over fear. Tara describes fear as something you cannot escape. What an amazing concept. Can you imagine how it would change things if we decided that fear is not bad or good, money is not bad or good, food is not bad or good? It's about the energy that we bring to those things.

If we can accept that fear is here to teach us something, show us something new, warn us and guide us, we can turn it into a useful tool and stop avoiding it.

What are you currently scared or fearful of? Can you surrender and have faith over fear?

Are you afraid to start that business? Are you afraid to quit your job? Are you afraid you won't have security? Are you afraid to leave a relationship that's not serving you?

For this Duality Dare, look at how you can operate from faith, and trust that fear will always be there for you.

Write down three things that scare you. For example, maybe you fear spiders, or maybe small dogs. Maybe you're afraid of what the scale will say in the morning. Maybe it's a fear of getting in a bikini.

Do something from that list that you are afraid to face. It doesn't have to be some monumental task. You get to start small. Maybe you decide to buy a new bikini and sunbathe in your yard. Maybe you're really afraid to have a conversation with your husband about the responsibilities in the home, so maybe you decide to talk with him today.

Sometimes we look at facing our fears as this big giant mountain we have to overcome right away. But what if, instead, you just accepted that you're always going to be afraid of that big mountain? And you get to do it anyway, because fear is ultimately your invitation into the next level of your ascension?

Surrender to that by starting with some less scary fears. Have faith that fear is for you.

CHAPTER 31

ENROLLMENT
NELLIE CORRIVEAU

Nellie Corriveau is a six-figure business coach. Eighty-eight percent of online women business owners are not making six figures, and Nellie is on a mission to change that. She helps women see selling as enrollment--as enrolling people into their vision, their dream, and their purpose.

People hire because they're stressed and exhausted. They're already successful, but they're stressed and making money or not making money, right. I come in, we have a lot of fun, and then the money comes.

Women get to make more money, and we get to have security. Money amplifies who you already are, but we've been conditioned to believe we shouldn't make money for centuries. It's bad to make money. It should be really hard to make money.

We get to throw all that out the window and revolutionize what women do, who they are, and what they're up to. It's going to take a massive movement of women standing in their power, owning their space, owning their gifts and their talents, and not feeling bad about charging their worth. You are priceless, but you also deserve to be compensated for your time and effort.

There's so much reprogramming that needs to happen. For example, many times, we say guilty pleasures, but the word guilt is in front of pleasure. So, reprogramming: it's not guilty, right? We get to break up with the word guilt in so many different ways and have all that pleasure, fun, and success.

Doing that permits the next woman. Think of that next woman that's watching you on social media. Standing in your purpose and your power gives other people permission and inspiration to do the same. Then they'll inspire the next woman.

HOW DO YOU DEFINE A MODERN WOMAN?

The first word that comes to me is authentic. It's still a newer term. We're still normalizing that it's authentic to show our feelings. For so many centuries, we've been told, don't cry because that means you're weak.

But the more authentic and vulnerable we are, the more connection we build with people. That's what I think of when I think of the modern woman--that person who doesn't try to pretend she has all of her shit together.

That drove me crazy when I was a new mom. I wondered, am I the only one losing it right now? No, it turns out. The same is true in business. Is this hard for anyone? Am I the only one that these things are not working for? Everyone's sharing all of their success.

I think success deserves to be celebrated, but we've got to share the behind-the-scenes. Doing that means you're being authentic and vulnerable because it's not easy to do.

IN WHAT AREAS OF YOUR LIFE HAVE YOU STEPPED OUT OF CULTURAL NORMS, DEFIED THEM, OR GONE AGAINST THEM? AND IN THOSE AREAS OF YOUR LIFE WHERE YOU'VE DONE THAT, HAVE YOU EXPERIENCED ANY SHAME OR GUILT, EITHER EXTERNAL OR INTERNAL? IF SO, HOW DID YOU MANAGE THAT?

A few years ago, I was a whole different person on the outside. The inside was fighting with the outside of that true, authentic self, trying to get out.

For over a decade, I built a super successful nonprofit from the ground up, starting at age sixteen. I had no money, no network, no clue what I was doing. But I had a lot of passion.

When you're running a children's charity, there are certain expectations. I thought I had to look a certain way. My hair was very long. I wore very conservative clothes, almost like the first lady. It was so far from me. No one told me to be that way, but I thought I had to be that way.

And the minute I left that identity, I went through much soul searching to figure out who I authentically am. My hair got shorter and shorter until I decided, let's just cut it off. It's also been purple. It's been every color. I've really enjoyed my natural color, too.

It's important to permit ourselves to change our minds. I cuss, and I get unfriended. People don't like me, and I'm okay with that. I always say, you're never going to make everyone happy, but are you happy? That's the most important part. We tend to live our lives for everyone else, but are we living them for us? Are we doing everything that we want to do?

You've got to listen to that inner voice. It's your inner compass, and it starts off as a whisper. We're so smart. We know all the answers if we listen.

177

HOW DO YOU TAP INTO YOUR DIVINE FEMININE AND WILD SIDE EACH DAY?

It's finding new challenges for myself. Every new level you get to, you're going to become comfortable at, right? Facebook Live used to terrify me. Now I can do it with my eyes closed. I also jumped in the snow, in a swimsuit, for charity, and it was scary. The snow was freezing, and the world could see my "whole me" in a bathing suit.

I also love being surrounded by other people, plus personal development, reading books, and listening to podcasts. Consuming all the good information and enjoying all the good people is what helps me.

Another thing I do is think about what's been on my heart. One thing I haven't tapped into yet is horses. I get to go horseback riding. I don't know why it keeps showing up for me. The same was true with ballroom dancing. A while ago, I said, I need to be on the dance floor; I need to dance. So it's just really listening to your inner voice, as we talked about earlier.

It's also the little things in life, like trying a new coffee, reaching out to somebody that inspires you on social media, and bridging that connection with people. I've met some of the most amazing people in the online space that I would have never met if I hadn't found the courage to step into who I was meant to be.

DUALITY DARE

Enrollment

Shifting the yucky "used car salesmen" stereotype so many of us have around the word sales is not easy to do. I don't think of sales as sleazy or icky anymore, now that I've shifted into using the word enrollment.

Nellie is the sales queen, but I personally would call her the Enrollment Queen. As a serial entrepreneur, I have gone from loathing "sales" to absolutely loving enrollment. Once we understand that "sales" is truly just enrolling another human into their vision, purpose, next level, and standing for their greatness, "sales" takes on a whole new meaning.

When we lead our businesses, our relationships, and even our own lives, and we start in our hearts and never in that icky "hook," we begin to understand that "sales" is an invitation for us to step into our next level of impact.

I want women to normalize the discussions around money and making lots of money--investing it, using it for the highest good, donating it, funding big missions with it, and creating generational wealth. Money is not the root of all evil. It is, however, the root of all big missions, big dreams and big movements. They all require funding. Money is empowering, and making it starts with leading from heart, never hook.

Money is an inanimate object. It is not bad or good. It is just the energy you put into it that creates the limiting beliefs around it.

For this Duality Dare, look at how you can enroll yourself into creating more money right now. Head to the journal section of the book and complete these exercises:

Step 1: What is the story you hold around money that might be preventing you from making and creating more of it?

Step 2: Can you find evidence that this limiting belief around money is false? For example, if you have a money story that money is hard to make or "doesn't grow on trees," can you find evidence in your past or someone else's story that will create proof that money is not hard to make? When have you seen money flow in your life or in someone else's?

Step 3: Write down three ways you can create money today. Don't know where to begin? Let's get resourceful.

Here are some examples:

1. Sell some of the things you no longer use on Facebook Marketplace

2. Start a book club and ask for a $10 membership fee to research and plan the books every month

3. Sell those beautiful scarves you make for friends and family on Etsy

4. If you own a business, call ten people you know today and enroll them into your offering, using heart over hook.

5. Going on vacation? Rent your house out while it's vacant on Homeswap or Airbnb

Step 4: Now, write down what this extra income, big or small, can do for you or your family. Over the next year, could you create more than enough money through heart over hook enrollment to go on a long weekend vacation to the beach and make lasting memories? Could you donate it to a local non-profit you love? Could you help subsidize your mom's medical bills? How can you connect to the difference you can make in another person's life when you enroll others with heart over hook?

How good will that feel? Now, anchor to the emotion you will embody when you create this in your life. This is how manifesting the next level of your life begins.

CHAPTER 32

CHEESE
JANET BARNETT

Janet Barnett has been a photographer for over twenty-five years. She's worked with a wide range of clients, including rock stars, executives, and entrepreneurs. Janet loves to help people pull out their best by giving them a picture of themselves they can love.

My mission is to be seen to serve. You cannot serve anyone in your client base unless they can find you--unless they can see you. Having a photograph taken is key to any entrepreneur on this planet right now.

Yet how many photos do women have of themselves that they love? It's probably a very small number. The number of photos they've actually taken the time to plan probably come down to their wedding and maybe a college or high school graduation photo. Sometimes there's a family photo, which is really about the family and not so much about the woman herself.

For any woman to just say, you know what? I'm going to have a photo session, and I'm going to do five or six outfits. I'm going to have a hair and makeup artist. I'm going to have a day for myself, and it's going to be amazing--that's a pretty big statement. I love women like that.

This is really about you personally. This is you getting in front of that camera and trusting someone. You're worth it, and it's one hundred percent worth it to have photos of yourself that you really love.

HOW DO YOU DEFINE A MODERN WOMAN?

A modern woman has a deep relationship with herself. She's very aligned with what she wants to do. Even if she's not doing it right now, she's got an idea of what she wants to be.

For me, it's definitely about doing your own thing, tuning out the noise, tuning out how you grew up, tuning out what your girlfriends think, what your husband thinks--to me, that's modern.

Accepting and celebrating yourself is part of having that deep relationship with yourself, which is one of many reasons I'm a fan of getting a photoshoot.

Many people whip out "practical considerations" as to why they can't get a photoshoot. "I'm too old. I need to lose weight. I'm too busy."

One of the questions I often ask entrepreneurs when they're starting up is, if I gave you a million dollars, what would you do with it? You're looking as good as you'll ever look. Your hair and makeup are done. You're wearing the best clothes you want to wear. What would stop you from doing this photoshoot if all those things were in place?

Even if life was as perfect as it could get, they'd still push back because they still don't feel they're worth it. Part of them thinks, "Who do you think you are to do this?"

I did a photoshoot in Paris, and let me tell you, I don't regret it for one second. I've got the most gorgeous images of me in Paris. I paid a lot of money for that photoshoot, and I booked an incredible photographer. It was a great experience.

As for "who do you think you are to do this?" I think I'm a woman who deserves to go to Paris and get a photoshoot. That's who I think I am.

IN WHAT AREAS OF YOUR LIFE HAVE YOU STEPPED OUT OF CULTURAL NORMS, DEFIED THEM, OR GONE AGAINST THEM? AND IN THOSE AREAS OF YOUR LIFE WHERE YOU'VE DONE THAT, HAVE YOU EXPERIENCED ANY SHAME OR GUILT, EITHER EXTERNAL OR INTERNAL? IF SO, HOW DID YOU MANAGE THAT?

I know people say don't look on social media. Don't compare yourself. I do look on social media, but I'm not looking there to compare. I'm looking there for inspiration. I'm looking for better people than me, who can give me some kind of inspiration to try something new or push it a little harder. That's really what I'm looking for.

You don't have to be the greatest at anything to be successful at it. You just have to be enthusiastic about it. I can still take inspiration from looking at other people's work--including work I think is better than mine--and still, be successful in my own realm.

This isn't about me, per se, but I think it's relevant to defying cultural norms. In the course of mankind, we've squashed down the voices of women, people of color, and other groups. Doing that has probably prevented diseases from being cured, books being written, plays being written, movies being produced, art being created, and the world being a better place.

We could have been so much further along if that hadn't happened. All that creative energy has been destroyed over time.

Now I feel like women, people of color, people of all gender identities are coming in strong, and it will be a different planet. "Cultural norms" are changing.

HOW DO YOU TAP INTO YOUR DIVINE FEMININE AND WILD SIDE EACH DAY?

My Paris photoshoot was very much tapping into the feminine. Everyone has that duality of the masculine and the feminine. Sometimes, when I'm in work mode, I'm not necessarily in my most feminine place. Sometimes, I may be listening to male coaches or entrepreneurs, and their advice may or may not resonate with me.

Then I'll listen to a female coach and think, oh yeah, she's right. We all need to be queens. We need to enjoy all the luxury we can and celebrate ourselves.

The funny thing about photography is that it's traditionally a very male-dominated business. It's very technical, and I was taught pretty much exclusively by men up until fairly recently.

But women are coming into this business strong because we have a different vision of how women should be seen. Even when I'm working on a shoot, sometimes I'm in my masculine, because I'm dealing with technical issues and organizational issues. Then when I'm connecting with the client, I'm more in a "girlfriend" energy. Plus, being creative in what I do is so fun.

I'm very easily influenced by pop culture and art. I'll open a new Vanity Fair magazine and be dazzled by an amazing shot. I'll watch a movie and see amazing lighting. Look at how the shots are composed. I can go on Instagram and just think, Oh my gosh, this is an amazing shot, I want to do something just like this.

DUALITY DARE

Cheese

I included Janet's interview in this book because so many women get lost in the image of what they think they should look like. I've done it, and I've worked with so many women who are paralyzed with fear when a friend or family member asks them to be in a group photo or pose for a picture.

My experience is that no matter how striking, fit, glamorous or seemingly flawless we think a woman is, they too have insecurities. I have worked with hundreds of women (many in the fitness industry), and no matter what shape and size or age they are, most have a low opinion of themselves. I was one of these women for far longer than I care to admit.

I was chained to the thought that my body and the level of my body's "perfection" was directly correlated with my self worth.

I think our sense of self and whom we think we should be in the world gets lost in the Instagram feed as we scroll endlessly through the images of "lifestyle porn," perfect bodies, and the flawless faces of youth. It would appear that no one except us has any imperfections.

Newsflash! No one looks like that. Let me repeat: NO ONE. Take it from me: I was knee-deep in bikini and fitness competitions and modeling for almost a decade. The dangerous lengths that I went to-- and so many of the other women I knew went to--in order to achieve that "healthy" body were outrageous.

We are our own worst critics. We scrutinize every inch of our body, obsessing about the tiny pockets of cellulite that no one else notices, the flaws in our skin, the way that we don't "match up" with the women on our IG feed. Sadly, we miss all the juicy moments, memories, pleasure, and joy in the obsession to obtain the unobtainable.

For this Duality Dare, I want you to become your number fan. I want you to see yourself for the divine, high priestess goddess you are, just as you are.

Step 1: Take a selfie (full body is preferable). Use a full-length mirror.

Step 2: Imagine yourself through the eyes of your best friend, sister, or daughter (aka one of your number one fans).

Step 3: What would she say about your photo? What would she say is your best feature? What would she say about your hair? What would she say about your style? What would she say about your smile?

Step 4: Write down all the things your number one fan would say about you in this photo.

Step 5: Every time your friends or family ask you to be in that group photo, mentally go back through this list, and stand tall, and then say...CHEESE!

BONUS CHAPTER

I know what you're thinking. "Jen, why is there a chapter about a man in a book about the duality of the modern woman?"

Many people take lifting women up to mean that we have to make men wrong. I do not see it that way.

We have more work to do before masculine and feminine are valued equally for exactly what they are, but that doesn't mean we cannot start celebrating them both now.

Alienating men will not lift women up. Leading by example, living as who you authentically are, and finding and using your authentic voice is what will lift women up.

I understand why so many women feel like they need to make men wrong for women to be right, but it doesn't need to be that way. Nor should it. That's not equality. That's trading one form of sexism for another.

We can be more than that. We can foster understanding between men and women. We can bring the duality of masculine and feminine to our lives to our world and enjoy the gifts each brings to the table. Like so many things we've already discussed in this book, it is not one or the other. We get to have both.

That's why I've added this bonus chapter with Richard Kavanagh. He's an incredible man who was raised by women and works in a female-centric industry. His perspective is exactly the kind that will help us create a world where men and women--where PEOPLE--are valued and celebrated, equally, for exactly who and what they are.

We're all humans, having a human experience, and we all get to be equal.

CHAPTER 33

EQUALITY
RICHARD KAVANAGH

Richard Kavanagh is a five-time Australian stylist of the year. He's an inventor, a visionary, a creative director and entrepreneur, and also the inventor of Peak, which is a revolutionary software system for salon professionals. Richard was raised by a single mom with a sister, and then became a hairdresser. He's been a man in the world of women for many years.

I grew up in rural New Zealand with a mum. My mum was only 16 when she fell pregnant with me, but she was a powerful woman and a great role model for me. She always had this ethos that you can be and do anything. You choose who you are, not society.

Whether you're a woman, whether you're a man, whether you're tall, short, slim, round--no matter what--you choose what you do. She ingrained that into me at an early age.

I grew up in the 70s, and as a kid, had no perception that women were ever not equal. They were always equals. People were people.

I was really interested at high school in art and science. I wanted to be a biochemist and I wanted to do art, but because I was an academic student, the school pushed me into academic subjects and wouldn't

189

allow me to do art. They would let me do the sciences and the languages and so on, but they wouldn't let me do art.

Through my teen years, I was a very naughty kid. I tried everything and ran way off the rails. It took me down some pretty dark paths.

I was also sporting a very punk look. My hair was cut into a bright orange wedge, with a flat top and pink and purple tips on a fringe that hung over one eye. The fringes were bright green.

This was 1983, so it was at the end of the punk era and into the new wave era. The girl doing my hair understood the chemistry and biochemical makeup of the components she was applying to my hair. She could predict a very measurable, scientific outcome through the processes of applying these chemicals to my hair. Because of that, she knew how to either augment or subdue the results of those colors.

She started talking to me about applying a very architectural, measured and mathematical approach to hair cutting. Hair is hundreds of thousands of flexible fibers hanging off an organic form. By applying architectural methods to it, you could create geometric shapes and patterns.

Hearing her describe this, it was as if someone hit me between the eyes with a hammer. I get goosebumps thinking about it even now. In every fiber of my being, I knew that I had discovered something I was meant to do even as a boy.

I grew up in rural New Zealand, in small towns, and I would go around to all these salons saying, "Hey, can I get an apprenticeship?" It took me a year of asking before somebody agreed to give me a go. I left school for my hairdressing apprenticeship and dove headfirst into a world of women.

I grew up with these great female role models. And then, I delve into a world of working with and being around women. I learned some things about women, particularly in the staff room, in the salon, on Friday night, when the girls would have a drink after work.

I would sit in the corner, wide eyed and absolutely shocked at the things that were coming out of their mouths. Not only did I grow up with a mother who was a very powerful woman and a great role model, but I also grew up with a stepfather who was very traditional in his sense of how you see women as a man. I was told that women didn't swear, use the bathroom, or fart, and I believed it. I thought that women were a different kind of creature.

THE POWER OF TRANSFORMATION

I want to talk about the power of transformation because I think that beauty and how we see ourselves in the world are so much more important than we realise.

In the modern world, the modern woman tends to have a kind of intellectual level, and we can easily brush aside appearance as shallow. It's not as important as entrepreneurial skills or academic prowess or business success, or sporting success. It shouldn't be given so much credence or credit.

But if we look in our hearts and look at how we feel, it's one of the worst things ever for women and men when you have a bad hair day. If someone gives you a shitty haircut, or they get your color wrong, or they style your hair in a way that doesn't feel like it's you or is not flattering to you, it impacts you at a core level. It impacts how you present yourself to the world and how the world perceives you.

I've had a really privileged career. I've been lucky to work with some incredible people, high-level celebrities, and big title magazines like Harper's Bazaar and Elle. I regularly work with a list of celebrities.

A celebrity I work with got a haircut from somebody else and sent me a message saying, "I don't know what to do about this. I don't feel like

I can go out in the world." She also said, "This feels so shallow. There are so many more people who have so many more problems than this. And yet, I can intellectualize that, but in my heart, I just feel like I can't face anybody. I didn't realize how important this was to me."

It's really important that you know you can be successful, you can be wealthy, you can be incredibly athletic, and you can still care about how you look. It's not one or the other. It's possible to be a walking dichotomy, right?

I have a lot of conversations with women, and I overhear conversations with women about so much duality. It's the challenge of working and being a mom, of wanting to be a mom but wanting to work. There's the fear of wanting to be an artist but also wanting to be a practical, pragmatic person.

For me, one of the easiest ways you can overcome this struggle is to accept the power of transformation and accept how looking good makes you feel good. I took all the gray whiskers off my face this morning and gave myself a little haircut because I feel better when I look good, and I feel shit with all my gray whiskers.

It can be so simple. It's little things like just go to the salon and get a haircut and get a blowout. That's all you need to do.

I was working in a small suburban salon in the early nineties, when I'd been hairdressing for maybe six or seven years. I was 22 years old and my first child, my oldest daughter, had just been born or was about to be born.

This girl came in to have her hair cut with me. I'd never met her before. She was a little overweight, she was incredibly shy, and she was wearing what I would refer to as perfunctory clothing. Clothes that covered her body but didn't really do much else. She had hunched shoulders, too, and a big port wine birthmark on her face.

192

Her hair was coarse in texture, and there was not a lot of it, so it was on the sparser side. It also had a bend that made it kind of awkward. If it were not styled right or not cut right, it would just be what you would refer to as bad hair, even though nobody has bad hair. It just hadn't been managed correctly.

She sits down in my chair and kind of picks her nails. I tried to talk to her about hair and her preferences, and she didn't have much to say.

I offered suggestions about what I would do, and then gave her a chic little bob with a sharp cheek line to strengthen her jaw line. I knew that I'd be able to blow dry that hair and make it look shiny and sleek by doing that. I gave a little bit of shape around the face so that she could wear it that way.

She wore it over her face so it covered her birthmark, so I cut it in a way that it could move, and give her that bit of protection, but still feel like hair.

This woman had the most beautiful, bright blue almond shaped eyes. They were easily her best feature. So I gave her this little heavy bang that just kissed the edge of her brow, so you could see those eyes.

Every time I tried to adjust her head so that her head was straight in the mirror so I could get the symmetry right, she'd look away each time she caught sight of her reflection. I just figured she was a shy girl.

After I finished her hair, blow dried it, gave it a little ruffle, and took the cape off, I looked back at the mirror to show her the line that I kept.

As she sat there, she finally looked up. She caught sight of herself, and she held her gaze in the mirror for about five seconds. Her spine straightened and her shoulders came back, and a smile spread across her face. She just sat there looking at herself like this. And

Then she got up out of the chair, kind of skipped over to the receptionist to pay her bill, flung open the door, and walked down the street, feeling transformed. It makes me emotional to this day. It's why I do what I do.

That's the power of transformation. The cut I gave her wasn't some crazy, wild, outrageous, incredible, magical thing. It was a haircut. Yet it changed that woman's day. If you're feeling shitty, go get a haircut.

How you feel changes how you turn up. At the end of the day, if you feel good because you look good, pardon my French but who gives a fuck? Turn up and be you. Be powerful. If being powerful means looking good, so be it.

It's a simple thing you can do. It's a simple thing to get your hair done; a simple thing to help you turn up, feel seen, feel acknowledged, and feel worthy of being seen.

HOW I CAN SUPPORT YOU IN YOUR NEXT STEPS

If you enjoyed this book, make sure you head to www.theduality ofthemodernwoman.com/gift to claim your free gifts: Full, uncut video interviews with every person featured in this book, and videos for every Duality Dare, where I expand on every Dare and share tips on how to implement them into your life, so you get the absolute most out of it this book.

If even one of the stories you read moved you, please use it to embrace your own duality and ascend, because embracing and integrating your duality is key to your ascension as a modern woman.

Your ascension into your authentic self, and a life that's authentic to you, is not fixed. It's a journey--a journey of evolving into a higher level of awareness and consciousness.

It's a continuous process of acceptance...accepting so you can then embrace. Acceptance is the first step to unconditional divine love, peace and harmony.

When I created an all-women's division of my company, I hoped that I could bring women together through "permission."

You see, I believe women have a long lineage of ancestral, generational, and cultural trauma and oppression we all carry.

I believe all the adversity we've endured creates immense empathy, and the divine feminine within each of us is the highest form of compassion and nurturing love, intertwined with endurance, strength, and sensuality.

As modern, in-demand women, I believe so many of us have forgotten who we are.

When I say permission, I want women to give themselves permission to be and embrace the duality and all parts of whom they get to be.

That includes permission to:

Be seen.

Be authentic.

Be vulnerable.

Be sexual.

Be bold.

Be heard.

Be transparent.

Be brave.

Be scared.

Be driven.

Be sensual.

Be nurtured.

Most of all, it includes permission to embrace our duality. Our duality is our power.

Our duality includes our connection to our feminine energy, which is the core of who we are. Feminine and masculine energy both live inside all of us.

The struggle I've had is leaning out of the masculine in my life, leaning more into the feminine, and realizing that pleasure is where I truly light up.

Our culture is so driven right now, and we're giving so many accolades to masculine qualities like the "hustle hard," performance-based ways of being. But I also feel things shifting, and I believe the shift we're feeling is the shift into healing--the shift into the feminine. The shift that is healing the imbalance of a culture that values the masculine and devalues the feminine. I don't believe this healing can happen in the masculine, and here's why.

Most of the time, women relate on a subconscious level in their trauma and their pain from a space of femininity. When they're feminine, when they're in that sensuality, when they're lit up and fully expressing themselves, when they're transparent and vulnerable, is also where they experienced trauma in their life.

I'm talking about sexual trauma. Molestation, rape, sexual assault, and abuse. Those traumas can often occur when women feel free and connected to their feminine ways of being, where they're creative and open. Not always, but even ancestral trauma and persecution historically occurred when women were stepping into their natural ways of being…when they were embracing their divine feminine goddess energy for healing, empowerment, protection, and their sexuality.

Historically, when women exposed themselves in these areas, they were persecuted or oppressed and labeled as witches, charmers, enchanters, magicians, or temptresses.

As we get older, it becomes more and more challenging to look at these past traumas and experiences. Looking at them takes us to some of the deepest, darkest parts of our soul.

Our subconscious doesn't want to look at the pain because it's terrifying. Our subconscious is designed to protect us, so it shuts down and avoids the terrifying darkness. Being fully immersed in your feminine includes being able to go to those dark shadowy places with eyes wide open. When you do this, you can alchemize and transmute the pain, darkness, and shadows into empathy, self-love, and light.

When our subconscious sends us into avoidance, that's into the masculine, where we put on our masculine mask. That mask keeps us "hustling hard" and keeps us from slowing down, and in doing so, prevents us from doing the deep shadow work that will allow us to set ourselves free by sharpening our sword and slaying those dragons once and for all.

And yet, to heal, we have to enable ourselves to be fully enmeshed in the feminine because the feminine is where we discover and unearth all the pain.

When we go directly to the pain, we can rupture the deep wounds, and in that messy, shadowy place, we heal. We transform the rupture into radical resilience. In that place is where our healing and the healing of all lives. We can once again shine and radiate our pleasure into the world like a ripple. The healing of one is then the healing of all.

We can't find our radiance when we choose to live only in our masculine energy. We can't turn on or turn up our light.

To be clear, the masculine serves a very important purpose. Neither masculine nor feminine energies are bad.

But we can't live in our masculine for too long, or it drains our energy and steals our joy. It takes our pleasure and drives us into overwhelm, anxiety, and depression.

When we fully show up in our feminine essence, ready and willing to go to the pain so we can have the light back, we get to turn ourselves back on.

That's where freedom exists, and that's when we can live fully in our duality, embracing all sides of us, including our masculine. We can go back and forth and do it from an empowered way of being.

I believe that the future is feminine. The power of duality is ours to harness, but only if we permit ourselves to fully embrace all sides of who we are without guilt or shame.

My mission is to allow women to share openly, authentically and in a safe space free of judgement. In the vulnerability of our own stories of trauma and adversity, we permit our sisters to trust that they can share their stories too.

Visit me and learn more about my mission at www.thedualityofthe modernwoman.com/gift so I can support you in your ascension, and in embracing your duality.

JOURNAL

_____

_____

_____

_____

_____

_____

_____

_____

_____

_____

_____

_____

_____

_____

_____

_____

_____

_____

_____

_____

_____

JOURNAL

JOURNAL

JOURNAL

JOURNAL

JOURNAL

JOURNAL

JOURNAL

_____

_____

_____

_____

_____

_____

_____

_____

_____

_____

_____

_____

_____

_____

_____

_____

_____

_____

_____

_____

JOURNAL

_____

_____

_____

_____

_____

_____

_____

_____

_____

_____

_____

_____

_____

_____

_____

_____

_____

_____

_____

_____

_____

_____

JOURNAL

JOURNAL

JOURNAL

JOURNAL

JOURNAL

_____

_____

_____

_____

_____

_____

_____

_____

_____

_____

_____

_____

_____

_____

_____

_____

_____

_____

_____

_____

_____

_____

_____

_____

JOURNAL

JOURNAL

JOURNAL

JOURNAL

JOURNAL

JOURNAL

JOURNAL

JOURNAL

JOURNAL

JOURNAL

_____

_____

_____

_____

_____

_____

_____

_____

_____

_____

_____

_____

_____

_____

_____

_____

_____

_____

_____

_____

_____

_____

_____

_____

JOURNAL

JOURNAL

_____

_____

_____

_____

_____

_____

_____

_____

_____

_____

_____

_____

_____

_____

_____

_____

_____

_____

_____

_____

_____

_____

JOURNAL

JOURNAL

JOURNAL

JOURNAL

JOURNAL

JOURNAL

JOURNAL